— *GOOD-OLE* —

ROTTEN APPLES

". . .by their fruits ye shall know them."
(Matthew 7:20)

ISBN: 978-0-7589-1029-5

Chick Publications
P.O. Box 3500, Ontario, Calif. 91761-1019 USA
Tel: (909) 987-0771 • Fax: (909) 941-8128

Outside the U.S. call for a distributor nearest you or see our entire
list online at: www.chick.com/distrib.asp

www.chick.com
Email: orderdesk@chick.com

Printed in the United States of America

CONTENTS

ACKNOWLEDGMENTS

I want to thank my Lord, Jesus Christ, who inspired me many years ago to write this book, and for sending good, Christian people my way such as Alfred Thompson. My husband and I met him many years before at a Youth for Christ fundraiser. He told us that things are not what you think they are. I have to admit it took some time for me, an old, stubborn, German Lutheran to understand what the Lord was saying through him.

"I would also like to thank the late Pastor "Cowboy" Ray Anderson. who prayerfully read and critiqued the very first "rough around the edges" manuscript I wrote many years ago, some of which has been incorporated into this book. I got to know him 14 years ago when he began working part time at the same place I work. "Cowboy" Ray was a Children's Evangelist, who traveled throughout the Midwest spreading God's word to thousands of children over the course of three decades.

More recently he graciously accepted invitations to preach at various churches that would find themselves in need of a pastor, never being interested in denominational lines, but rather wanting to see the Gospel proclaimed in every church. The last sermon he was going to preach was a sermon about Rotten Apple Christians, but he went to be with Jesus the day before he was going to preach it. At his funeral his son preached that sermon. Ray's sermon notes were all ready to go, written almost as a script, along with all the necessary props. It was almost as though Ray knew he wasn't going to get to preach this sermon, but he wanted someone to. In the sermon he used an object lesson that demonstrated how a perfectly good, flawless apple can be rotten to the core.

Similarly, we can be the best little Christians to the world and behind closed doors we may be saying things we shouldn't, watching things we shouldn't, reading things we shouldn't — sinning without remorse or repentance. With God's guidance, Ray's son did a great job. Needless to say it brought tears to my eyes thinking how, years before, Pastor Ray always encouraged me to continue writing, no matter what.

Of course I would also like to thank my family for their prayers and patience and understanding.

You will find, in some parts of the book, that an English major I am not. This book is written as if I was speaking to you personally —my heart to yours. So you English teachers, please disregard any grammar mistakes that you may find yourself wanting to address.

INTRODUCTION

The story centers around the third chapter of Genesis, where God made it very clear to Adam and Eve that they could eat of the fruit of the many trees in the Garden, but there was one tree that He said to stay clear of. The fruit on the tree looked good, inviting, and luscious, but if eaten, it would turn rotten to the core. God called it the tree of the knowledge of good and evil. Even in my Sunday school days I had heard about the story of the snake in the tree infecting the good apples.

Little did I know, from a little child on, that God was lovingly teaching me about real evil spirits. But to me it was just another Sunday school lesson.

As I grew older and more into "religion," this personification of evil became a red cartoon character, with a pitchfork and horns, that children and adults would dress up like on Halloween. Never did I ever hear a sermon on Sunday morning about real demonic spirits from the Bible, and what they have done and can do to someone, without them even knowing it.

The pastors just kind of skipped over those verses. I guess

they thought those lessons were only from Bible days, or just not important, or they didn't fully understand them and didn't want to tackle them.

As I grew older and perceived to be much wiser, I just knew that, if by some rare chance, demonic spirits still exist at all, they could only be in voodoo witch doctors in Africa somewhere. Never could they ever come near me or my family.

NOTE: Let me stop right here and say that this story is in no way, shape, or form to glorify Satan, but instead to expose Satan and his devils, and to make innocent, vulnerable, deceived, *religious* people, like I once was, aware of who Satan and his devils are and what they can and are doing behind the scenes.

I didn't know that real demonic spirits existed. Mark 5:8-9; Luke 10:18-20, and Colossians 1:13 show that they are real and are evil. In 1 Peter 5:8, demonic spirits roam about through the earth seeking whom they can destroy.

Matthew 10:1 shows that they are unclean. Matthew 8:29-32, Mark 5:1-13; Luke 11:24-26 show that they are spirit beings without bodies that can inhabit a body. 1 Timothy 4:1; Revelation 13:12-15; 1 Corinthians 10:20 show they spread false doctrine, have power to work miracles, and they encourage idolatry which is the worship of many false gods. Matthew 12:21-30 shows that demonic spirits are under the command of Satan. John 10:10 shows that Satan comes to steal, kill, and destroy.

The demonic world wants to destroy every living, breathing person on the face of this earth simply because they are made in the image of God. One would have to have his head buried in the sand to miss the sheer existence of demonic spirits. They have started wars, attacked the home, the family, education, governments, churches; murdered millions of unborn babies in the mother's womb; interfered with human sexuality and the marriage relationship.

All anyone has to do is just open up any newspaper or listen to any news on T.V. and you will see how demonic spirits work behind the scenes. And then someone might say, "Well, that person just comes from the other side of the tracks. It will never happen in my family."

If that's so, then how can it be explained when a child that comes from a good, loving, church-going family, that gets good grades, very well liked in school, takes a rope, and strangles himself. Or they get drunk at a party, and on their way home have a fatal accident, and kill themselves and a family. You hear about an honor student, good in athletics, who doesn't think twice about blowing someone's brains out.

Sometime in their lives they unknowingly or willingly chose to open up a very small door to an evil spirit, which is addressed in this book. Then they are capable of even the extreme of what demonic spirits are capable of making a person do, such as a man in Florida who literally chewed the face off another person. A psychologist would refer to this as losing all sense of reality or someone might say he just went off the deep end.

So demonic influence can come in many different ways and levels, many times without people ever knowing how dangerous it is to open that first door. And I am not saying to look for devils behind every bush, but I am saying that we just need to be aware there is a spiritual battle for our souls and we need to know how to deal with them.

Satan wants all people, from all sides of the tracks, to be sick, deceived, drunk, drugged, destroyed, and dead. We need to realize that Satan's tactics are nothing new. He is still doing his dirty work. The Word of God says in 1 Peter 5:8: "Be sober, be vigilant; because your adversary the Devil, as a roaring lion, walketh about, seeking whom he may devour."

And of course this devilish spirit doesn't come with a big, flashing sign that reads: "I want you broke, busted, and deceived, or sitting on your blessed assurance in your nice, comfy, cozy, church." No the Bible describes Satan as being transformed into an angel of light. (See 2 Corinthians 11:14.) And what person doesn't grow up believing that all angelic beings are from heaven? I know I did.

There are so many good, caring, people, that have very innocently taken the bite of the sin-laden forbidden fruit and some don't even know it. My heart goes out to these precious people with a compassion that is indescribable.

You will see, as you read this book, sometimes the same message is repeated, but in a different setting in the next chapter. Maybe that's why the Lord has so many good parables and key doctrinal words and verses repeated in the Word of God. Sometimes I had to hear and read the same message over again in the next chapter before it finally started to make sense.

So now, as it says in Isaiah 1:18: "Come now, and let us reason together…" as I share with you what God placed in my heart many years ago.

The title of the book is, what else, but what the serpent fed Adam and Eve, and what Satan is spoon-feeding the world every day, described in Isaiah 5:20, that evil is good and good is evil, that forbidden fruit those… "Good-ole rotten apples!"

1

ADAM AND EVE TAKE THE BITE

In this chapter, we imagine that we are a fly on the wall of the headquarters of Rotten Apple City.

One of Lucifer's devils from the devil patrol came running and yelled. "Get to the Garden, now, God is talking to someone, I think he called her, 'Eve!' It's serious!"[1]

So Satan wasted no time. He quickly transported himself to the Garden of Eden, just in time to see God walking with Eve in the cool of the day. God was showing her all the beautiful trees as He said, "Now Eve, this is very important. You can eat of the fruit from any of these trees, but there is just one fruit tree I want you to stay clear of. It's the one over there in the middle of the garden."

Satan quickly turned himself into a serpent, and had it all

---

1) The usual term, "demons" does not appear in the King James Bible. When Jesus cast evil spirits out of a person they were called "devils." In this book, we have used "devils," instead of "demons," where possible.

planned out exactly what he was going to say to Eve. Now some may think the snake really didn't talk to Eve. But there are many animals that can talk. What about our fine feathered friends the parrots who talk very fluently?

So Satan slithered his way up to the very top branch as he heard God tell Eve, "It's the tree of knowledge of good and evil. I gave you a free will to choose and I have planted this tree here for you to learn right from wrong. But you have to choose to make the decision for yourself. You are going to have many experiences where you think something seems good and right, but it really is not."

("Woe unto them that call evil good, and good evil; that put darkness for light, and light for darkness; that put bitter for sweet, and sweet for bitter!" —Isaiah 5:20).

"This is very serious, Eve, because if you choose to eat the forbidden fruit from this tree you will die. You will have chosen to be separated from Me and My protection. It's your choice. It's entirely up to you."

Satan watched carefully how she was going to handle this. For a moment, his heart sunk, as she turned and walked away from the forbidden fruit tree. But then it happened. She turned and walked back. Satan watched as she hesitantly kept edging her way closer and closer to the tree. And then, in curiosity, she just touched one of the twisted, crooked branches.

Satan jumped for joy as he thought to himself, "She just gave me the green light to move. Even though she didn't touch the forbidden fruit, she touched what's connected with it. She is curious, and that's all I need to get her started. If God is going to get in my business, then I will get in His. He may be the God of heaven, but you can bet your ever-loving apples that I will be the god of this world." (2 Corinthians 4:4)

"Eve is so naïve she won't even realize it's me. I bet I could even turn myself into an angel of light and she wouldn't know who I really am." (2 Corinthians 11:14)

Satan slithered closer to Eve and quietly whispered. "Pssst. Hey Eve! Over here. I can see you are very frustrated. I can help you."

With some degree of relief Eve said, "Oh, I sure hope you can. God told me I could eat the fruit from any of these trees but this one. God said if I willingly took the fruit from this tree and ate it I would surely die."

Without a moment's hesitation, Satan quickly said, "Oh, I think you heard Him wrong. You see, I just happened to be strolling along in the Garden, minding my own business, and I just happened to have overheard your conversation. Now I wasn't trying to Eve drop or anything. I wouldn't do anything like that. But I did hear what was really said. I distinctly heard God say that you could eat of all the beautiful trees, including this one. You won't die."

At that point Satan thought he had her, but he could see she was a little hesitant. So, being the father of lies (John 8:44), he added some more lies and deceptions. He said, "What will it hurt if you just try it? God would never deprive you of eating fruit from any tree including this one, now would He?"

Eve was still not sold on the idea, so Satan had to keep lying as he said, "You know what, Eve? When you take a bite of this fruit your eyes will be opened, and you will gain much knowledge, and you will be as gods, knowing what's good and what's evil."

But Eve was still hesitant so he had to go on a little further,

"Please come a little closer and just feast your eyes on this beautiful, luscious fruit. I know you are hungry. Go ahead! It's okay. God wouldn't care."

Eve reached out and touched the apple. Satan said, "Now pick it off the tree and take a bite." Eve took it off the tree and just looked at it for the longest time. So Satan had to keep going with his lies and deceptions.

Satan thought to himself, "I don't give up easily. I am not going to let this one go." He said, "Look, Eve. It's good for you. It will make you wise. Surely God wouldn't want to withhold such *benefits* from you."

Little did she know that she would be far from wise and knowledgeable, she would be naïve and vulnerable. The knowledge that Satan would give her would lead her to trusting the false gods of Satan's world, making many wrong decisions, —even eternally wrong decisions. That's the ultimate goal of Satan's crowd, but as you can see, Satan's crowd has to keep making it enticing for you at first.

Satan thought to himself, "I must get her to take a bite, because if she doesn't, then she is honoring God and God will bless her with the gift of discernment to be able to tell what are really some good apples and what are some bad apples." Satan insisted, "Look Eve, this is just food for thought. What do you have to lose? I know you are hungry. Just take one little bite. For heaven's sake, you're not going to die! Just do it!"

Satan thought, "Hey! I like that saying. JUST DO IT! Don't concern yourself with the consequences, JUST DO IT!"

So Eve thought about everything Satan had said, and without thinking about it any further, she did it! She took the bite. Even though it left a funny taste in her mouth, she just ignored it. And after a few more little bites the funny taste grew less and less and pretty soon, the funny taste was gone altogether. She wanted more and more. She just couldn't get enough.

She couldn't get enough of that good, ole, rotten apple. Now, she couldn't keep this to herself, so she quickly picked all the many different kinds of apples off the tree and put them in an old, rickety apple cart.

"And when the woman saw that the tree **was good** for food, and that it **was pleasant** to the eyes, and a tree **to be desired** to make one wise, she took of the fruit thereof, and did eat, and gave also unto her husband with her; and he did eat," Genesis 3:6.

She ran with the apple cart to where Adam was and shouted. "Adam, you gotta try these apples. They are to die for. Here take a bite!" Satan was so excited he started dancing and singing:

Some are really big!

Some are very small!

Some don't have any spots on them at all!

Some are really shiny!

Some look almost round!

But the one that I make Adam pick will be rotten apple brown!

Adam thought only for a moment and he picked what he thought was the best one in that cart and he took the bite. It seemed to leave a funny taste in his mouth. It just didn't taste so good. In fact it tasted horrible. And then it started burning. No matter how much he tried to spit it out, it kept burning. And then it happened. A really strange feeling came over both of them. They had a sickening feeling of regret, a knowing in their hearts that they had both just made the worst decision of their lives. They disobeyed God.

They felt so ashamed, they ran. As they were running you could hear them say to each other, "Why did you make me do that?"

"It was the serpent. He made me do it!"

"Oh yeah, right! Did he shove the apple in your mouth?"

"No, but he made it sound pretty, good, and inviting!"

"You could have said no."

"Well you could have, too!"

As they continued to argue, they ran. They ran so fast you would have thought they were on fire. Their hearts were pounding and pounding. They kept running trying to hide themselves.

And then they heard a loud, thunderous voice from God, "Adam, where are you?" Now God knew exactly where they both were. But he directed His question to Adam because he was supposed to protect her from danger. When God said, "Where are you?" He meant: "Where are you now, spiritually?"

Satan's eyes were as big as saucers. With an evil grin, he rubbed his hands together and thought, "I've got them now. They are mine, all mine. They can run all they want. Spiritually they are mine. Now I have the green light to bless Adam and Eve with spirits of jealousy, lying, cheating, pride, hate, rebellion, and even murder. And maybe I'll just throw in for good measure the spirit of lust. Hey, the sky's the limit! And what's even better, they will bless their children with the rotten apple family tree."

Satan grinned, "Oh, this is sweet! Because of Adam and

Eve's sin, everyone on the face of this earth will be born into sin. They will all have a sin nature. They will all have a salacious hunger for the good ole rotten apples. I love it!"

How does the Bible describe the situation, now?

Romans 3:23: *"For all have sinned, and come short of the glory of God;"*

Romans 5:12: *"Wherefore, as by one man sin entered into the world, and death by sin; and so death passed upon all men"* Matthew 7:20: *"Wherefore by their fruits ye shall know them."*

And the forbidden fruit was passed to the third and fourth generation over and over and over and over and over and over and over again. (Numbers 14:18)

So, with this beginning, mankind, you and I, inherited a sinful nature, which has continued to give ear to the lies that the enemy and his helpers whisper our way. Let's imagine how this plays out, again from the view of the other side.

2

ONE LITTLE THOUGHT

"Wow! It's almost midnight, the bewitching hour," Satan proclaimed. "Time sure flies when you're having fun! I am famished. All this talk about rotten apples. Let's take a break and have a little bite to eat and de-stress, while our stress devil says a few words about what he has been assigned to do. I am sure there are twists and turns everywhere."

The stress devil paraded up to the front and exclaimed, "Let me tell you there are not only twists and turns, but ups and downs, and highs and lows everywhere. So with that said, I have found, through much trial and error, what works best to stress people out, is, I set people up to make them fail. I find their weak points and study them. It may be that someone said something to them that hurt them. It may be their parent was not there for them emotionally. It may be they had a tough day at home or work or school. It may be from a traumatic experience from the past or present that in some cases I kinda help along a little.

"The Bible says in Ezekiel 38:10: 'Thus saith the Lord God; It shall also come to pass, that at the same time shall things come into thy mind, and thou shalt think an evil thought.'"

"Evil thought," Satan said with a smile. "Oh! Please tell me more!"

The devil continued, "It all starts with *one little thought* that I pop into their minds. The Lord is warning people about these evil, negative, thoughts, and if they don't know how to deal with them they can lead to even more negative, evil, thoughts. We all know THOUGHTS DETERMINE DESTINY.

"I am so glad that people do not take to heart what the Bible says in Romans 12:2: 'And be not conformed to this world: but be ye transformed by the renewing of your mind, that ye may prove what is that good, and acceptable, and perfect, will of God.'

"Notice the words *"renewing of your mind."* I am so glad that most people were never taught how to renew their minds from evil or negative thoughts. This makes my job so much easier. Now, as soon as their stress level starts rising I start watching what they gravitate to.

"And if their weakness is food, then what magically pops into their mind is, 'I know you're tired; that was a tough day. Wouldn't that sinful dessert, that double-fudge-chocolate brownie, dripping in ooey-gooey, scrumptious, frosting taste really good right now —wouldn't it just hit the spot? Wasn't that awful what happened to you, I know you're hurting. Why don't you just go and have one right now, it will take your mind off what happened. It will make you feel so much better!' And I let them chew on that a while. And pretty soon they start to salivate, and they salivate some more about that brownie, until the saliva is running out of their mouths.

"And then another thought pops in their minds: 'Oh for heaven sake, just go and eat it.' So they pop up off the sofa and out to the kitchen and then, like magic, another thought pops in their mind, 'It's not that big —just one is okay.' Sometimes they try and talk themselves out of it. I hear thoughts coming from them like 'I'm okay. I can handle this. I don't need to eat right now. Maybe I'll go for a walk; maybe I'll just find something healthier to eat.'

"When that happens, then I have to take it a step further, 'Oh, it's too much work to get your shoes on and go for a walk. But that ooey-gooey brownie sure would taste good. You don't want that healthy snack and big drink of water. It's not going to satisfy you. Have just one little brownie, instead.' And then, finally, they get the plate out and cut themselves a small brownie and they take one small bite and then that brownie is history.

"And then another thought pops in their mind, 'That was so good, now have another. Just do it! This is making you feel so good. Don't worry, be happy, at least for a while.' And then while they are eating, I waste no time in popping the thought in their minds, 'Oh, this is really good. I think I'll have one more. Just one more isn't going to hurt. I could eat the whole pan, —well, maybe I just will.'"

"And they keep eating and eating and eating. Then a little bit later another thought pops in their minds, 'You're still hungry aren't you? Maybe something crunchy this time, how about some chips.' When they have eaten half the bag then another thought pops in their minds. 'You might just as well finish the whole bag.' Pretty soon they get a sick feeling in their belly and they finally stop eating.

"Then I mix the good, bad, and the ugly with just a touch of guilty thoughts: 'It's okay; you can start again tomorrow. Why did you eat that? What else are you going to graze on? Can't you just control those cravings? You are pathetic! Now you blew it! You might just as well eat some more. Wasn't that awful what happened to you?' Then I add some more thoughts: 'You will feel better if you just have a little something more to eat. No, you better go and exercise and go for a walk. No, not today, maybe tomorrow. You couldn't just go for one little walk?'

"So as you can see, my ultimate goal is to set them up to fail and turn them into junk-food junkies that have to have that next guilty, pleasure-fix to get high. And of course, when it's dinner time, that *one little thought* is that another big helping will not hurt.

"Now with some people it may not be food that they crave, no matter how much I encourage it. So I have to find a different way to get them relaxed or feeling high.

"Usually it doesn't take much. Just that *one little thought* I pop in their minds like something is not right here... have a drink or take a drug... smoke a joint or chew some tobacco... beat someone up... talk about them... have an affair... or buy a new car... watch another dirty movie, or play a video game... or just shop till you drop. And they either act on those thoughts or they can fight those thoughts all they want but eventually they give in and we get the glory. It all can be so, so addicting and it's all so wonderful.

"You can see the smile come on their face and the stress just melt off their bodies —at least for a while. But then, I am happy to say that, in a few days, that *one little thought* pops back into their mind and the same deceptive cycle starts all over again.

"Sometimes I tease them with the thought: 'This is money you are spending foolishly;' or 'This junk food or one more trip to the bar is not good for those already-clogged arteries, and pancreas and liver.' But I make sure that those thoughts are removed very quickly.

"Sometimes this whole process takes a while. Each person is unique and different. Sometimes I make them so miserable and depressed that they want to make themselves throw up what they just ate. Binge and purge, binge and purge, and no matter how skinny they get, even if they are almost like a skeleton, they look in the mirror and I make sure that they see themselves as fat and ugly as I whisper in their ears, 'There still is some fat on you. You are pathetic.'

"Sometimes all I have to do is pop *one little thought* and they take over from there. But sometimes it takes several. It just depends on what's going on that day. But it's not only 'the thought' that counts, it's the stress we can put on them because of that *one little thought* that we pop into their minds.

"And the granddaddy of them all is to just make them feel hopeless. There is no hope. I keep drilling that thought into their minds until they just give up completely. And I let them chew on that for a while. I get them really down in the dumps and blue. I call it my no-way-out blue-plate special. No way would I ever want them to know *there is always hope in Jesus*. That's *one little thought* I would never pop in their minds."

3

RELIGIOSITY AND WITNESS AT THE COUNTY FAIR

Now that we see how this Rotten Apple thing got started, let me show you how it played out in my life. In my small town of 4,000 people, everyone looked forward to the county fair. But after I became a Christian, the highlight of the fair was always when the Transport for Christ, Chaplain Dave and his wife Laura, had a church service the very last day and you'll never guess what Bible Chaplain Dave preached out of.

Let me give you a clue. It has the seven-letter "Saviour" with U in mind. Not one key doctrinal word has been removed. It glorifies the Lord Jesus Christ 100%. It has been burned and destroyed many times and has stood the test of time for 400 years. It's the only Bible that has earned the right to have the words "Holy Bible" stamped on the front cover. It has God's certified seal of approval. Of course, it is the Authorized King James Holy Bible.

The Sunday morning service was always held in a tent that was set up for activities throughout the week for the fair go-ers. But then one year they moved a country church building into the fairgrounds and the services were then held there. It just so happened that that very church was the little country Lutheran church that I grew up in.

It was a little bit strange walking into a church that I hadn't stepped foot into for too many years to mention. A flood of memories came back to me with each step I took. I shared with Chaplain Dave my memories of growing up in that church, and of my testimony, how I later accepted Jesus as my Lord and Saviour.

He asked me if I would share this with the congregation. I didn't know what to say. I was seeing people come that I knew. But some I had never seen before. They came in and sat down in the very pews that I remember sitting in as a little girl. I was a little nervous, but the Lord gave me a prompt and the peace that passes all understanding came over me, and I said that I would.

I began by telling the people in the church that my ances-tors helped build the church. I pointed to the big, old, black stove and told them that, in the winter, we always went to church early so Dad could get the fire going, so by the time church started it was at least partly warm. I pointed to the pul-pit and told them my Sunday school class was at the bottom of the steps up to that pulpit. Another class was behind the big, tall, altar. Another was in the back of the pews. We were all jealous of the younger kids, because their class was around the big, ole, warm, black stove.

It wasn't long when Sunday school was over, and the church

bell rang and we took our seats. Everyone tried to sit as close to that old stove as they could to keep warm. I would shiver as a cold breeze came over me from the window. But when I scooted over to my Mom and tucked my arm under the arm of her furry-warm, brown coat, I felt better. I can remember the feeling of curling up close to my Mom's pride and joy, that warm, brown, fur coat. She wore that coat everywhere, even to get groceries.

I pointed to a corner and said that the old pump organ stood right there. The organist would play her heart out as everyone sang those great ole-time hymns. The pastor's sermon echoed in the church, lulling me off to sleep.

When I got a little older, Mom let me sit in back by the older kids. When people would come in from outside, we all laughed as the pews creaked like they were going to break as they sat down. We waited with baited breath as the organist would hit a wrong note and we would giggle. More than once I saw my Mom and a couple others turn around and give us "the look."

Every Sunday we would count how many old ladies had dyed their hair. As the sun peeked through the tall, skinny windows, some of the ladies' hair seemed to be almost a gray-ish-blue. At this, I could see smiles come on the ladies' faces. I continued saying that sometimes those ladies' hair was really blue, as blue as blue could be. The laughter broke out and echoed all over the church. Even Chaplain Dave was laughing.

I told that how, when church was over, we all took turns trying to climb up the big, thick, scratchy, rope that rang the church bell way up inside the steeple. Sometimes we could get the bell to ring and ring. We ran around the graves playing tag, which of course was very wrong, with Mom and others giving us yet again "the look." No one really disciplined their children in public, you just got "the look" and you knew you better cool it or you'd pay for it when you got home.

As I continued speaking, the people seemed to be more relaxed, and I felt God helped me relax right along with them. Now I had their attention. Smiles of joy seemed to be glued on their faces, wondering what funny story I would tell next. But what I was about to share with them next was not funny at all, it was very serious.

I could feel what God wanted me to say. For a moment I froze, and then God's peace again came over me, and I was able to continue. I pointed to the baptismal fountain. It was beautifully carved in mostly white with little brown accents. As I was looking at it, I thought about the Ten Commandments in Exodus 20 that the Lord gave to Moses. I had learned every one of those commandments in that very church. The Lord said "Thou shalt have no other gods before me. Thou shalt not make unto thee any graven image…." In the dictionary "graven" means, a carving representing a god.

As I pointed to the "graven image" I told them that that was exactly where I was baby baptized. For years and years, I kept the white handkerchief that Mom had given me one day, that the pastor used after he sprinkled water on my forehead, baptizing me. Of course, my Mom and Dad and my brother and sister were right beside me. The pastor then would turn to my appointed godmother and he would ask her if she would make sure I would be brought up in this theology, to which she would respond, "I will."

I pointed to the round, wood altar with the maroon kneeling

bench. I said that this is where I took communion many times. I was not confirmed in this church. I took classes with other church kids in a big Lutheran Church in a town nearby. To this day I still have my old, gray, Lutheran catechism handbook where I learned all about my Lutheran religion.

I can remember as if it were yesterday, parading up to the front of that big church with my confirmation class. We all had white robes and red roses pinned to our lapels. Each of us said a little speech and then the pastor asked us "Do you accept Jesus Christ as your Lord and Saviour? Then answer 'I will.'" To which our whole class in unison replied "I will." And then the pastor said, "And do you renounce the Devil in all his ways? Then answer 'I will.'" And again we all said, "I will."

Our parents came up and we all took communion at the altar. And then we were given a certificate and we had our pictures taken individually and together as a class. I will never forget the look on Mom's face. It was a look of relief that now this was over and I did what I was supposed to do and I was going to be okay.

Then I paused, and very humbly said, "But I am here today to tell you it was not okay. Did I really accept Jesus as my Lord and Saviour? No. Did I renounce the Devil in all his ways? No. The baby baptism and the confirmation were nothing more than a hand-me-down religious tradition. The Lord even warned people in the Bible about manmade, religious traditions."

Their smiling faces turned to somber faces.

For the first time in my life I noticed what religion can do to a person. I noticed some ladies sat up a little straighter in their pews. Some just stared at me. Some looked a bit angry.

Like the saying goes, baptized in pickle juice. Many of the ladies were giving me "the look" that I so well remembered my Mom gave me in my younger years. I am sure they wanted to get up and walk out but didn't quite have the nerve to do it.

I told them that I had accepted Christ only recently. I realized I was a sinner not saved by grace, but a sinner that needed a Saviour. I needed Jesus. Not just a Sunday morning Jesus, but an everyday, personal relationship with Jesus. I repented of my former lifestyle and surrendered my life to the only One who could save me, that could give me peace. It was Jesus! The Bible says that "Jesus is the way, the truth, and the life."

I could see by "the looks" that I was getting, that they didn't have the foggiest idea what I was talking about. In one of the pews towards the back, I noticed that there was a lady whom I had never seen before who was wiping her eyes. The more I talked, the more she quietly cried. I don't know what happened, but I give God all the glory for whatever He did to that lady's heart that morning.

I then continued by asking them a question: "Now, how did I know that I truly had accepted Jesus Christ as my personal Lord and Saviour and that it was not just lip service again? Because, I noticed that, when the very next time that I took communion, it took on a whole new meaning."

And let me stop right here and talk about that word "communion." It should never be called "communion." It's the Lord's Supper. When we call it "communion" we take the Lord out of it. So now that I had given my heart to the Jesus, the Lord's Supper took on a whole new meaning. That little cracker represented Jesus' body being beaten and broken for me and for my sins. Like the Bible says, "...this do in remembrance of me." And before I drank from the tiny little cup, I kept staring into it. The dark juice seemed to be shimmering in the glass.

I felt a tear run down my face. It gave me goose bumps as I thought about the pain and suffering Jesus had while hanging on that cross and it was all for me. I realized this was not just another Sunday ritual, it was a time, an important time, a very special time, to remember what Jesus had done for me. Now John 3:16 took on a whole new meaning, "For God so loved the world…," —that's me and you! "For God so loved the world that he gave his only begotten Son, that whosoever believeth in him should not perish, but have everlasting life."

As I am writing this now, I can remember before, when I took the Lord's Supper, it was just another lip-service, moment-in-time, as we all marched up to that very altar. The pastor would hand us the tiny glass of wine and the wafer and we would quickly chew up the wafer and down the wine.

The Bible reads, in 2 Corinthians 13:5: "Examine yourselves, whether ye be in the faith; prove your own selves. Know ye not your own selves, how that Jesus Christ is in you, except ye be reprobates?" Did I think about the sins I had committed that week before and did I have a little talk with Jesus and ask him to forgive me before I took the Lord's Supper? Was I even saved? No way! But remember, I supposed that I was a "sinner saved by grace." And I had my fire insurance ticket to heaven through infant baptism.

I am ashamed to say I concentrated more on the wafer getting stuck in the roof of my mouth than where I needed my heart to be, and that was with Jesus. I would hear the pastor say, "Your sins are forgiven, now go in peace." That is another fallacy. No one has the right to declare to another their sins are forgiven. That's between you and Jesus. And we would march back to our pews, and the next bunch would march up to the altar and the same thing was done.

As I got older and attended other churches, the little oyster cracker would be passed around in the pews. The pastor would give a long speech that really meant nothing to me. I can remember to this day how I would see people around me eat the cracker, then quickly their heads would bob back as they took the drink. Just like myself, there were people looking all around. It wasn't two seconds later and I heard the click, click, click of people's tiny communion cups, including mine, as they were all placed in the carved-out holes specially made directly in the back of the pew in front of me. There was never any time to reflect on what this all meant. It was: "Well, what's next."

Now that I had truly accepted Christ, He wasn't just someone I prayed to, reading a ritualistic, man-made prayer in the front of our hymn books, singing the same liturgy Sunday after Sunday. It was a prayer that I prayed from my heart. I didn't have to read it out of a book, and then say the same words, "hear our prayer," and "also with you," over and over again. (Matthew 6:7 KJV: "But when ye pray, use not vain repetitions, as the heathen do: for they think that they shall be heard for their much speaking.")

And as time went by I noticed some changes were happening in me. I didn't want to listen and watch dirty movies and shows on T.V. I didn't want to listen to a dirty joke or hear swear words roll out of good, caring, people's mouths that I had never heard before. Some would end it with "pardon my French," while others just went on with their conversation. I didn't want to go the places I had gone many times before.

And serving the Lord was not: "Oh, do I have to?" Now, I wanted to serve the Lord. I had a strong desire to.

Little did I know at the time, way back when, that that strong desire was to expose the very thing I was talking to these men and women about, Religion.

I told the people in the church that day that when I truly accepted the Lord, and acknowledged Him as the Lord of my life, the most important change happened and the litmus test whether I was truly saved or not was that I had a heart for the Lord like I had never had before. I had a heart for the deceived, for the lost, for the unsaved. In fact, one time I had a dream about innocent, caring, good people walking slowly into the fire of hell, and they didn't even know they were doing it. I thought about what it says in Jude 1:23. "Save them from the fire."

Now I really hit a nerve. Now I was treading in deep religious waters. I could see the wheels in their heads turning. I could tell by "the look" I was getting they just didn't understand why I was talking the way I was. I said, "Church is and always was meant to be a place to worship the Lord, to equip the saints, to be soldiers in the army of the Lord. Not a bless-me social club."

When I finished sharing my testimony that day and walked back to my pew, the lady that had been quietly crying all the way through my testimony, stood up, said nothing, but held out her arms and gave me a big hug. People were staring at us, and giving me "the look" and I didn't care.

When the church service was over, all the religious people walked as fast as they could out the back door. The lady that had given me a hug, didn't say anything to me. She waited till everyone left, and then got up slowly and quietly walked out, too. Only a few people stayed and shook my hand and gave me some positive comments. I said it wasn't me. It was the Lord that gave me the words to say. I give him all the Glory.

I left the church that day with mixed feelings. I was on a spiritual high, knowing that the Lord had done some spiritual surgery on a few hearts that day in my very own little country Lutheran church. To God be the Glory. But at the same time I was angry at how deceived these religious people were. It wasn't their fault. Like the movie, "Fiddler On The Roof," It was tradition, tradition, tradition.

As you can see by reading the Good Ole Rotten Apple Story, it's all about exposing Satan's deception and lies any way I can. And I will continue to expose the rotten apples he has thrown at me, and convinced me and my family to take a bite.

4

FOOTPRINTS
OF THE DEVIL

When I was growing up, my father was an alcoholic. My sad, teary eyes were fixed on the big ole grain truck going down our long driveway, which meant Dad was going to town again. That would only mean he would come back with more cases of beer. In the middle of the night I would come down stairs to go to the bathroom. And there was my drunken Dad in the kitchen in his striped pj's weaving back and forth at the counter having a little bedtime snack.

But come Sunday morning, dressed in his Sunday best suit, Dad was the first one there to open the door to the old country church and get the old black stove warmed up. I would look over at him singing the old gospel songs thinking just a few nights ago this guy was so drunk he could hardly get the bologna, sardines and cracker sandwich to his mouth.

There were many nights when Dad's drinking ended up

with Mom and Dad yelling at each other. I tried hard to study and do my homework over the loud noise with whatever was happening downstairs, but gave up and cried myself to sleep. The next morning coming down from upstairs for Mom's good bacon and eggs breakfast, I could hear Dad snoring loudly. When I got to the bottom of the stairs where their bedroom was, the strong, lingering, liquor smell felt like it was burning my nose.

I had a hard time concentrating in school, thinking about what was going on at home. Always wondering when Dad was going to get drunk again. Was it going to be worse the next time? I wanted to get good grades. I tried hard to stay awake, trying to listen to the teacher or take a test. But, the dreaded report card always revealed the worst to me: C's and D's and sometimes red F's.

In those days you didn't get just an F but a red F on papers and report cards and Satan was right there with that "one little thought" —your Dad doesn't love you. That's why he drinks. And those red F's: "Boy, you are really dumb; you are never going to amount to anything."

Now, with some kids they can go through something like this and even worse and whiz through school. Sometimes Satan leaves them alone, at least for a while. But then, when they least expect it, the Devil comes like a roaring lion seeking whom he may devour and it all starts with that "one little thought" that leads to more until he has them and they don't even know it. For me the Devil didn't let up or shut up. "Sins of the fathers visited to the third and fourth generation," Exodus 20:5.

When I became a teenager, following in my father's and

grandfather's and great grandfather's footsteps, and so on down the generational line, I started drinking, too, staying out till all hours of the night. After one particular drinking party I was held down and raped by four boys. With what I went through with my father and then the horrible rape and of course the puppy love breakups every teenager girl encounters, the Devil tried to put that "one little thought" in my mind "men are horrible, why don't you find another woman?" But, by the grace of God I didn't listen to that evil, deceiving, lying spirit. The Devil is the father of lies. (See John 8:44.)

I was married in 1967. Every Saturday night we were both at the bar religiously. But when I found out I was going to have our first child I quit drinking completely. My husband continued drinking more and more and became very emotionally and physically abusive. In the morning I could smell that all-too-familiar smell of lingering liquor in our own bedroom that I smelled when I would pass by my parents' bedroom when I was just a little girl.

My husband was a real Jekyll and Hyde. Really sweet to me outside of the home but in his drinking binges didn't think twice about picking up a lamp and throwing it across the room at me. One day my husband took care of our baby so I could get some groceries. As I was getting out of the car I could hear our baby screaming. I ran to the nursery and saw my husband violently shaking him. Little did I know at the time that by violently shaking babies you can actually kill them. I didn't know anything. Our marriage certificate or birth announcement didn't come with instructions.

Little did I know that the only instruction manual I would ever need for anything was in the last place Satan would ever want me to look: God's Holy Word. But in our home, the Bible was no more than a nice decoration on the coffee table with some old antique granny glasses on it.

Sometimes, after my husband's violent behavior, he would apologize and say he loved me and was so sorry he didn't know what got into him. I know now what got into him. It was a real demonic spirit that was literally controlling him, like the Bible refers to in 1 Peter 5:8.

He could go for weeks without getting violent and then the least little thing might set him off. I thought, maybe, if we had more children things would get better. We had one more little boy and then a little girl. And things were pretty good, for a while. In fact, he even quit drinking. But little did I know he just traded one addiction for another. He became what I would call a dry drunk, type A perfectionist.

He went to the Mayo Clinic School of Anesthesia in Rochester Minnesota and graduated 2nd highest in his class as an anesthetist, one who puts people to sleep in surgery. Of course, with the money he made, material things were the most important thing in his life. He traded his addiction of drinking for another new sports car and boats and lots of boy toys, all to make himself feel better. The Bible says the love of money is the root of all evil. (See 1 Timothy 6:10.)

At the hospital Christmas party he would only mingle with the rich doctors and their wives. I will never forget at one particular hospital Christmas party, one of the doctor's wives, dripping in diamonds, turned to her husband and said, "Love, light my cigarette!" I thought I was going to throw up. I looked at my husband, he was grinning from ear to ear. It didn't upset him in the least. It was at that point that I realized how fakey and phony she was and many others at that party, also. So I quietly slipped over to the table where the nurses and cleaning ladies were sitting and the rest of the evening I had a great, fun conversation with them.

When we got home from that party, my husband was furious with me. I tried to explain that I just didn't care to be around such phony people, but he just didn't understand. And with glassy eyes he didn't touch me, but threatened me with the words, "Don't ever let that happen again." And from then on, even though he never hurt me again physically, the emotional abuse was just as bad. My life was always waiting for the next shoe to drop. We lived in very nice homes. He always picked the house we would be living in and of course new furniture. I had no say so whatsoever.

He would let me buy things to accessorize the new furniture, and didn't even say anything when I would put that same Bible with the antique granny glasses on a brand new end table or coffee table. But the only time I touched it was to pick it up and dust the table. That Bible was a treasure chest of all the instruction and information I would ever need placed right in front of me and I didn't even know it. It reminds me of when Pontius Pilate was standing in front of Jesus asking him what is truth; and with loving eyes the Truth was looking him right in the face, and he didn't even know it.

We moved over 20 times, because he would get mad at someone at the hospital or he would flat out get fired from his job. My Mom would always say she was running out of room in her address book to put our new address. He was never satisfied where he was. There was always a better-paying job at a different hospital.

I was the one that would always have to explain to the children that we were moving again and again and again and again and again. I can still see the big moving van backed up to the house while the children watched with such a bewildered look on their faces. They would make friends and then have to leave. They would have to get used to yet another new school.

And things never changed at home. If the children accidentally spilled their milk they were made to feel like they were worthless. But it was nothing for him to deliberately throw a glass of chocolate milk on a beautiful, very expensive couch. I was so angry at him but didn't dare say anything, thinking it will only make matters worse.

Our mentally challenged daughter, who he had very little to do with, was hit and swore at just for accidentally dropping a plate on the kitchen floor and breaking it. It was nothing for him to walk by and slap her hard on the back of her head and call her dummy.

One day I had had enough and I threatened to leave him. He said, "Don't ever try it. I will take the children and you will never see them again." And in those days there were no safe shelters to go to. I couldn't go back to live with Mom and Dad, with Dad being an alcoholic. So I lived in constant fear, day after day, wondering what would happen next. One day he was out of control and the next he was half-way decent.

Like I said earlier, he was a real Jekyll and Hyde. On one of the better days, he came home with a cute little brown puppy. One day we were giving the puppy a bath. It was not a fun time. He was swearing at me telling me to hurry up, even though I was working as fast as I could wash him. The puppy could sense his anger and turned his head and nipped him. He picked up the little puppy and opened the front door and literally threw him outside. Then he stormed into the bathroom and got a Band-Aid for the little bite mark on his hand.

I ran outside and wrapped a towel around the puppy. He was yipping uncontrollably. I put the hurting little puppy in the car and took him to the vet. The puppy ended up with a broken leg. After that, when that little puppy would see him, he would run and hide. I felt sorry for the puppy. He was scared to death just as I was.

And Satan was right there with that one little thought: "When is the next shoe going to drop... when is it going to happen again... things will never get better, they will only get worse. Why don't you just kill yourself! After all, what hope do you have?" I didn't know there is always hope in Jesus. I didn't know *Jesus is the answer*. But at the time the answer I needed most was the furthest thing from my mind.

And as far as church goes, he would always tell the children, "Why do you want to go to church? It's not going to do you any good!" So eventually they quit going. I kept going, but always ended up sitting in the back, crying. But with each new move, I got so I didn't want to talk to the neighbors or try and find a good church anymore because I knew it wouldn't be long and we would be moving again.

School came easy for our boys. But when they came home with all A's and one B on their report card, instead of their dad saying, "Great job. I am proud of you," they were grounded for a week for that one B.

Having to move to yet another new school, I could see they were becoming distant. I didn't blame them. One day I had to go to the principal's office because my older son was really getting out of hand. The counselor suggested he should see a therapist. I totally agreed, but when I mentioned that to my husband, he went ballistic and yelled, "He don't need no shrink and don't you ever mention that to me again!"

In 1987 my husband had a 5-bypass, open-heart surgery. After that, he became extremely depressed and from then on was very quiet. No more horrible beatings or negative unloving discipline did the children experience. He just sat in his Lazy-Boy chair and stared at the ceiling most of the time. Can't you just hear that "one little thought" from the Devil: "Why don't you just kill yourself. Everyone will be better off without you."

His mother told me later that his own father had 9 heart attacks, and at the age of 45 he died. That had to be so devastating to a young child watching that happen with Satan whispering in his ear over and over again: "You will never make it past 45."

Following in his father's footsteps, at the age of 45 my husband committed suicide in a motel not far from where we lived. Don't tell me the Devil is not real. Like the Bible says, he goes around as a lion seeking whom he may devour. (See 1 Peter 5:8.) His mission is to rob, kill, and destroy, and that's exactly what he did to my husband and our family.

From that day on I was left all alone with my 3 precious children. Needless to say, I was devastated. I went back to church every Sunday thinking that this has to be the answer. I would sit in the back of the church and tears would come to my eyes and I would run out of the church. My children and I just existed —trying to make it through another day. When my children needed me most I had nothing left to give. I was emotionally drained. The Devil had me right where he wanted me. In fact, one night I heard "one little horrible thought" that Satan popped in my mind, "I got your husband and your Dad and I am going to get your children!"

The very next day I went to my undiscerning, liberal, (religious), Lutheran pastor. I told him my concerns. He didn't give me any comfort whatsoever. He didn't even open his Bible once. He referred me to what he called a Christian therapist who he said could help me sort things out. I was so desperate for peace and answers I thought I would give her a try.

5

————————

A TOUR
OF THE NEW AGE

I liked her right away. It seemed like the more she talked the more comfortable she made me feel, even though she suggested and said things to me that I had never heard before. She said I needed to clear my mind and meditate on "the light." I said, "What light?" And she said, "It will take a little time but you will see it." This so-called Christian therapist never mentioned Jesus to me once, but what did I know? I was trusting that my pastor knew who he was sending me to.

Little did I know at the time that this was not a Christian counselor but a religious, New Age guru. She was, what I learned later, a white witch. She was not dressed in a black cape and pointed hat. She was dressed very "normal" and respectfully. I was opening myself up to occult practices and I didn't even know it. And the worst part of it was, I loved it.

She had me come to see her twice a week. She gave me

books to read and tapes to listen to at night to meditate on and relax me. One day she told me about a really good seminar coming up called the mind-body-spirit connection, in a city about a hundred miles from where I lived. She said it would really help me further my spiritual healing. I didn't even hesitate. I signed up, paid my hefty fee —and went.

When I walked into the room I was greeted with a pleasant smile and was then escorted to my assigned seat. The room had lighted candles that created a very pleasant aroma. I asked the person next to me if she had ever been here before and she said many times, and each time she learned something even more wonderful than the time before.

Part of the subtle deception of these seminars is that these people come from all walks of life. I was told that one of the Zen/teacher/gurus was a very prominent surgeon's wife. Everyone I came in contact with had a peacefulness, a calmness about them that I wanted. I thought, "I feel so good, what can be so bad about all this." Oh what deception!

At these, what I now call cultic, New Age, workshops, the instructor told us we had come to the right place. She said we would learn how to manage stress and sort out past painful experiences and manage any situation that comes along and forever be at peace. I thought, "Oh man! That's what I want. That's what I am looking for. I really am in the right place." Oh how deceived I was!

She said, "It all starts with the "Christ consciousness." I thought, "This must be okay because she just mentioned the word Christ." I didn't know any difference. Then she said, "And from there you need to carefully, gradually, slowly, tap into your particular spirituality," (which is really a fancy name for demonology). But I didn't know it. At that point I remember some people got up and quietly left. I was thinking, "Why in the world would they leave? This is just getting good.

I didn't have the Lord Jesus in my heart. I didn't have the Holy Spirit discernment to tell me to get out of there. The Devil had me so convinced that this is just what I needed. Give me more. The teacher saw the people walking out, and quickly told us that they were not ready yet, they will be back and escorted us into another room.

There were no chairs, just mats on the floor. We were told to sit on the mats and just relax. She then showed us a picture. It was huge.

She said, "Every one of you here today have seven energy centers aligning your spine. They start from the base of the spine to the top of the head and are referred to as your seven light chakras. She then instructed us quietly to lay down on our mats, close our eyes, relax, and focus on those lights inside our bodies. Soft music started playing in the background. The instructor again told us to relax and empty our minds and focus on the lights. She said this several times and then she stopped talking. It was quiet. I could hear the beautiful, soft music playing.

I wanted so much to have peace in my life, I did everything she said. It wasn't long and I was feeling the warm feeling from the top of my head to the base of my spine. My body almost went limp, I was so relaxed. From that feeling on I was hooked.

Biblically speaking, this is pure devil worship. Following anything other than the one true and living God for answers is idolatry. (See Deuteronomy 32:17; 1 Corinthians 10:20.)

After that first seminar I got on their mailing list and went to as many seminars as I financially could, all over the country. Some seminars made me a little uncomfortable for a few moments as we were all told to clear our minds and chant the words, "As Above —So Below," over and over again. What I did not know is that this is one of many ways to call in evil spirits. But the instructor always mentioned the "Christ consciousness" so it must be okay.

Again I saw people getting up and walking out. But not me. I was in my glory. Notice I said in MY glory. Not glorifying the Lord Jesus Christ, but in my glory. That's what New Age is. It's very self-centered. It's all about me; finding the answer within me.

When the seminar was over, people, including me, were clamoring to the tape tables to buy some so-called relaxing music tapes. We couldn't get our money out fast enough. Every seminar always ended with an overwhelming feeling to buy something we just knew would help us even more.

After a few months I felt confident that I could conquer the world. I thought, "I don't need the so-called Christian counselor anymore. I am fine now." I couldn't get to the book store fast enough to get another book or tape that I could listen to, so as not to lose the wonderful feeling I was having.

I didn't know it at the time, but the Devil was spoon-feeding me a bunch of garbage —those good ole rotten apples— and I loved every morsel. I watched videos and read books by the world-renowned psychics, Sylvia Browne, and Marianne Williamson and her New Age "Bible": "A Course in Miracles." I practically devoured these books and many more. And the New Age guru that was featured on many talk shows, Deepak Chopra —he was my idol.

I can remember feverously scanning the newest *TV Guide* for talk shows that would have yet another new age guru on that I could record on my old VCR. One day Oprah had the movie star, Shirley MacLaine, on. She was promoting her latest video. Of course I had it. She told Oprah about the seven light chakras and how wonderful they are. I knew them well. I was glued to the T.V. She had the whole audience doing some so-called relaxing meditation, and of course, me included.

I started getting deeper and deeper into this way of life. I needed more and more to satisfy me. I never could have enough of these very expensive mind-body-spirit-connection seminars all over the country. But then something happened.

I was at work and just doing my usual meditating, focusing on my light chakras that I learned from Shirley MacLaine's video, "Inner Workout," when a fellow worker of mine came up to me and said, "Judy, I really care about you. You have no idea what you are doing." I was very offended at her and asked her what she meant.

She said, "When you clear your mind in the dangerous way that you have been doing, you are opening yourself up for any spirit to come in. Please don't do this." She explained to me in detail how her brother did the same thing. She went on to say with tears in her eyes that it seemed so innocent to him, but the more he dabbled, the more he liked it, and it almost ruined his life.

At first I was mad at her. I thought to myself, "What does she mean 'any spirit to come in?' I just don't understand. How dare she talk to me like that. Her brother just didn't know any better."

I went to bed that night, like I had for years, with my headphones on listening to my so-called "relaxing music." I woke up the next morning not feeling good at all. I threw up several times, and decided to stay home from work. I was lying on the couch flipping through the channels on the TV and the Montel Williams Show came on. And who did he have on that day but Sylvia Browne. She was a very familiar figure in my life. I had read many of her books. I was glued to the TV. I loved it. She was so fascinating; she talked about everything I had learned in my videos and books and expensive seminars that I had gone to over the years.

That day, Williams made an announcement that she was so overwhelmingly popular that she would be a regular on his show every Wednesday. The audience cheered and clapped with excitement —me included. So, needless to say, every Wednesday, I taped Montel's TV show so I could watch her when I came home from work.

One Wednesday eve, I was watching her and I heard her talk about the Ouija board being a portal. For some reason that word "portal" stuck in my mind.

There was a young lady by the name of Heather who was having some weird things happen in her home, and was trying to get some answers from a Ouija board. Things got worse. Thinking it might be the Ouija board, she decided to destroy it. She tried to break it in two. It would not break. Tried to burn it and it would not burn. There was a spirit that took over. Her friend, Sue, said her eye color even changed. I was on the edge of my seat wondering what would happen next. That's how hooked I was on this deception.

Finally the great Sylvia proclaimed, "I don't want anyone to mess with a Ouija board. They are the most dangerous things! Talk about a portal." She said, "What you need to do is sprinkle salt around the house and ask for the *Christ consciousness.*"

("Red flag!") There was that word "Christ" again. Those words and the word "portal" seem to make me uncomfortable.

Then one Wednesday eve I was watching Montel again. This time there was a couple on the show by the name of Oscar and Jennifer who said something was in their house. Sylvia said they had an entity in the house by the name of Charlie. They asked Sylvia if Charlie was dead and she said no and nothing can go through anybody and *nothing is a portal. So give that up. That's goofy stuff."

There was that word "portal" again. But this time, instead, I heard her say, "Nothing is a portal." I couldn't believe what she was saying. I thought maybe I heard her wrong so I played back that part of the tape and sure enough that is exactly what she said: "...AND *NOTHING IS A PORTAL.* SO GIVE THAT UP! THAT'S GOOFY STUFF."

I thought to myself, "Now wait a minute here. Something is not right here. I thought I heard Sylvia talk about a Ouija board as a portal. I then played that video about the Ouija and her exact words were: "TALK ABOUT A PORTAL." I thought: "That seems strange. One time she talks about something being a portal and then in another show she says there is no such thing as a portal."

I usually just taped over TV shows that I recorded, but now I know God had a different plan. I still have some of the original videos which I have since taped onto DVD's.

On one show I caught her again talking about a portal. This time she was talking about an ENERGY IMPLANT OR A PORTAL that was in her bedroom. But why, then, did she tell Jennifer and Oscar: "Nothing is portal, so give that up —that's goofy stuff."

After that happened, I thought I needed to pay closer attention to what she was really saying. So every Wednesday I was sure to tape Montel's show. Sure enough it happened again. On one show she stated that A BEACON IS ALMOST LIKE A PORTAL. On another show she encouraged a lady's young son to talk to the spirits and her last comment was: "You are not going to let in the PORTAL OF EVERYBODY." On another show there was another lady named Felicia talking about her experience with the Ouija board. This was the conversation:

Montel: Oh! Here we go talking about Ouija boards.

Sylvia: I'm telling you this: I don't know how many times I've had to say this: please don't mess with Ouija boards; they are really evil.

Montel very seriously says to the audience: Let me tell you something, this woman has been on the show with me for 16 years. The very first time I spoke with Sylvia Browne, sitting outside of the Queen Mary, the third thing out of her mouth as we were talking about ghosts and spirits was: "Those Ouija boards! I hate those things. People —They're crazy. They need to stay away from them."

Sylvia makes a face and says the word, "Evil."

Montel, on the edge of his seat, says: What is it that makes them so evil? Who created the Ouija board anyway?

Sylvia: Oh, it goes back so far; they are actually French; they used to call them plashets. Ah, and the thing about it is that… what happens is… it's almost… see, the Ouija board… well you know how we talk about portals… are almost a portal.

Montel says to the girl: Leave it alone!

Sylvia: Leave it alone. I'm telling you, I wish they would burn all of 'em. I don't care what —they're just bad.

So here Sylvia is telling this lady, Felicia, that a Ouija board is almost like a portal. But referring back to Jennifer and Oscar, Sylvia told them: "…nothing is a portal; so give that up —that's goofy stuff."

On another show, (this really took the cake), Sylvia told a lady to ASK GOD TO REMOVE THE PORTAL. And as Montel and the lady were talking, Sylvia would interrupt several times with: ASK GOD TO REMOVE THE PORTAL. But why, then, did she tell Jennifer and Oscar that nothing is portal, so give that up, that's goofy stuff?

There is yet another show where I caught her lying, this time about the word "VOODOO." A lady says, "I'm living in this old house and there are people or spirits just dancing around. I just want to know their names. I need to talk to them."

Montel is freaking out: "Wait, wait, wait, wait, wait!"

As I was listening to Sylvia explain her comments to the lady, I noticed how Sylvia's words and sentences seem to be all jumbled together. Her eyes were shifting up and down as she was making it all up.

This is what Sylvia said, word for word, to Montel as he is freaking out: "NO NO NO No No No, this used to be… ahh… and please don't let this upset you, because voodoo isn't what people think it is, but this used to be where people who practiced voodoo… ahh… you know, stayed. Now please, people think that voodoo is nothing but putting pins in dolls, no no! voodoo or voudon is very, very spiritual… the true, so… yeah, you do have them. It's like Mardi Gras."

The lady, now, really smiling and convinced, says, "Yeah, it's party time."

Sylvia comes back with: "I know, all the time!"

The audience laughs.

So this show she is telling the lady, voodoo is very spiritual and in the next show I watched her comment that voodoo is "crazy crap."

On this particular show, a lady says, "I deal with the dead a lot, and they keep giving me messages for everybody, and everyone thinks I am crazy, or a witch, or something like that." Can you tell me if I am spiritual?

Sylvia quickly responds "Why sure you are. And, you know, I always say, I am only as good as my last reading. If you're getting more valid than not, for God sakes, keep it up. But every morning ask to make sure it comes from God. Ask for the *Christ consciousness,* (red flag) the Holy Spirit to surround you. See what I am saying? But don't mess with anything that is voodoo or Ouija boards and all that crazy crap. We don't need that."

Before, Sylvia's expression was to make the previous lady accept voodoo. Now Sylvia turns up her nose weeks later and calls voodoo "crazy crap."

Little did I know that I would catch the great Sylvia Browne in one lie after another for months. To this day I still have some of the original videos that I copied onto a DVD.

I was told years ago to take them to the media like "60 Minutes" and have them aired publicly.

On another show she makes up some ridiculous lie about spirit guides. She says a spirit guide may take some time training to be someone's personal guide. What Sylvia is not saying is that the devil is learning the weak, vulnerable parts of a person. This devil may not rear its ugly head for years, but then, one day, out of the blue, when you least expect it, he closes the trap. 1 Peter 5:8 warns us that the Devil goes around like a roaring lion "seeking whom he may devour."

On another show, a lady asks her what her animal totem is. Sylvia answers, "Your animal totem is a cheetah." Montel responds quickly with: "Explain what this is all about so everyone will know what you are talking about… an animal totem is." Sylvia quickly responds with: "Everyone has an animal that protects them."

So, that is her explanation of whatever an animal totem is? Again, is this another lie she just made up? Could it be that she made up these words, "animal totem," so she and her son, Chris, can make up a book called "Animals on the Other Side"? Oh! She's good!

One day she said she put a tape recorder in Bela Lugosi's house and, with a really weird look on her face, said, "You should have heard what I heard."

Whether she did or did not realize it, she was actually listening to devils. She is dabbling in things that are very, very, dangerous.

When she says that someone's deceased loved ones are right behind them, or that they actually had 30 past lives, that is a lie from the pit of hell. There is no in-between. What she is seeing and hearing are demonic spirits masquerading and mimicking as their dead loved ones.

The Bible calls these familiar spirits and says to stay away from them. A necromancer is someone who talks to the dead and it is forbidden in scripture.

On another show a lady says, "I come from a line of seers and one night I was awakened by what sounded to be like a dozen birds just flapping wings. Could you tell me —was that my angels that I heard?"

Sylvia responds with her eyes shut and says, "Yes, but don't say seers,' say 'psychic.' Otherwise we will get into Deuteronomy where it says don't consort with seers or sorcerers. So don't. If you're psychic, you're psychic. If you're a seer, you got spells and cauldrons."

Sylvia doesn't like Deuteronomy. Hmmm! I wonder why? Deuteronomy 18 warns people they should have nothing to do with a charmer, or a consulter with familiar spirits, or a wizard, or a necromancer. "For all that do these things are an abomination unto the LORD."

One day, on Montel's show, a lady was talking about how she must have, somehow, opened up a door to a demon, because there were some real, strange, things going on in her life. A real red flag to me was the way Sylvia responded to this poor, desperate girl. She rolled her eyes, almost mocking the poor girl: "Listen! For the hundredth time —there is no such thing as a demon! There is certainly evil people, "dark people" we call them... We have really dark spirited entities but there is no demon. Just use the sign of the cross and holy water and salt all around the house, and you will be fine. And remember —there is no such thing as demons, honey."

What blasphemy, when Sylvia is dabbling in the demonic world, to tell someone demons don't exist and to "use the sign of the cross and holy water and sprinkle salt all around your house."

In another show Montel is commenting to Sylvia, "You

know, when people call you, most people are looking for something spiritual. But I also kinda get this idea that people might get into anything that might pass their way." Sylvia interrupts: "See, that's what scares me is… during this time —and I talked to someone on 48 Hours, and I won't mention who it was— you have to be so…but during this time you have to be so careful about getting into anything occult. Because of the breakdown of some of the religious norms and dogma, people will start following these goofs. And then you will get a Jim Jones and everybody will start drinking Kool-Aid."

Montel: "Do you expect to see any of that?"

Sylvia interrupts: "Yeah! I am seeing it in L.A., I am seeing it in a lot of places; that people are putting these people up as saviors. And that is so wrong, Montel! That is so wrong!"

Note: What about how Sylvia, who is being idolized as a so-called "savior?"

Montel is saying that wherever he goes, people come up to him and say, "Uh, I really like your show, but, Ah! —I love Sylvia!"

People in her audience are saying, word-for-word: "I think you're fantastic. I have read all your books. I honor you! It's such an honor to talk to you. Your words are such a comfort to me. I love you, Sylvia." When she makes her grand entrance at the beginning of Montel's show, she always gets a red-carpet welcome.

On what is called a "Montel moment," Montel talks candidly to the audience before Sylvia makes her grand entrance. He is talking about Sylvia as he says, "Our friendship is far different than you would imagine it to be. We don't spend a lot of time talking about psychic stuff. Sylvia is like my sister."

On one show, Montel introduced Sylvia Browne as the "heavenly" Sylvia Browne. Then Montel says, "I like that. — the Heavenly, Sylvia Browne."

My heart goes out to these good, caring, but deceived people because at one time they unknowingly opened up a door to a very dangerous spirit. I know where they are coming from and it grieves me to see this happening to them. I just want to run up to them and put my arms around them and tell them I care about them and beg them to get out of this deception now before it's too late! Just the little bit I dabbled in witchcraft, I can see how inviting and intriguing but deceptive it can be. Satan doesn't come knocking on people's doors telling them he wants to eventually destroy them. No! He makes himself look real good, sometimes for a very long time.

"And no marvel; for Satan himself is transformed into an angel of light." (See 2 Corinthians 11:14.)

At times, it almost seems like it was Sylvia's show, and Montel was the guest every week. I don't know how many shows I have watched where Sylvia interrupted Montel and made him or an audience member feel very inferior, like she could tell anyone anything and they would believe it.

On some shows it was very obvious that she was making things up. She would stumble through her words and sentences, look up at the ceiling, roll her eyes, or she would put her long, witchy, hook nails in her mouth!

Another time, a lady shows Sylvia a picture that she took from an airplane window that looked like Jesus in the clouds. Sylvia's response: "Some people may see Jesus, but my guide just told me it's an angel; it's an archangel. They fly with us all the time. I mean, when we are flying, they fly with us. Then you don't have to make the sign of the cross 15 times while you are in the plane."

One day Montel was promoting one of Sylvia's books called "Lessons for Life." She talked about an 8-step programs and she said "If you do it (and *I don't usually guarantee it)*, but if you do it right, in 8 to 12 weeks it will absolutely change your life."

I noticed that Sylvia sneaks in *"I don't usually guarantee it"* And the audience and Montel never catch this. I wouldn't have either if I hadn't been on to her.

She says she is from the good side —from the light side. Well, my Bible says that Satan comes as an angel of light. (See 2 Corinthians 11:14.) Light or dark, it really doesn't matter if it is white witchcraft or black witchcraft. It's all the same. It is very, very dangerous! That's why the Lord warns us in the Bible not to have anything to do with it. (See Deuteronomy 18.) But we are to reprove or expose it. (See Ephesians 5:11.)

I noticed that many times people will ask her about some dead relative and if that person is okay and happy. Sylvia comes back with: "Of course they're happy, honey. Why wouldn't they be?" Sylvia plays on their sympathy and tells them exactly what they want to hear.

On another show she encourages a lady to increase her spirituality and Sylvia says, "By increasing your spirituality — guess what? You start to see things. You see, years ago, they tried to separate psychic and spirituality which is wrong and it's all the same thing. It's a cell phone from God. So they are just coming to say hello —welcome."

In another show a lady says, "I tell these spirits to go and sometimes they do and sometimes they don't. I think I am experiencing astro catalepsy because I read your book."

Sylvia: "Yeah, listen to me. Call on Lilith."

Lady: "Lilith"?

Sylvia: "Yes Lilith, cause she is the governess of the lower levels; *we call* the governess of the lower levels."

Note: She is saying right here that she knows about the lower levels when she says: "We call on the governess of the lower levels."

I just about threw something at the TV when this show came on: A lady asked Sylvia "Is Heaven here?"

Sylvia "Yes! Heaven is three feet right up off the ground, right here"

Montel, looking so puzzled and confused, says, "So, everybody is walking around…?"

Sylvia: "UH, HUH! RIGHT HERE! So we are ghosts in their world."

Montel looked even more puzzled and confused.

Sylvia: "I told everybody at a lecture one time that you had almost turned white when I told you *that* about Heaven being three feet off the ground."

Montel: "I know! That was kind of tricky."

Sylvia laughs.

Even a small child knows where the real heaven is, and it's not 3 feet off the ground. Just another one of her made-up lies.

Many times she does talk about "god." Which god is she talking about? There are a lot of gods in this world. She also talks about the Christ consciousness. That is a term that I learned when I was heavy into new age and the psychic phenomena. It has nothing to do with Jesus Christ. Being in New Age for many, many years and being trained in psychic phenomena, every show brought back horrid memories of what

I was once hooked into. I know firsthand what I am saying! Sylvia Browne is a real con artist. I have been where she has been, I have done what she has done.

Sylvia said that it is important to light candles because spirits don't see regular lights, but they do see candles.

1 John 4:1 warns: "Beloved, believe not every spirit, but try the spirits whether they are of God: because many false prophets are gone out into the world."

Leviticus 19:31: "Regard not them that have familiar spirits, neither seek after wizards, to be defiled by them: I am the Lord your God."

Familiar spirits are demonic spirits. Those attempting to contact the dead, in Bible times and even to this day, have a spirit guide who communicates with them. These are familiar spirits. Leviticus chapters 19 and 20, and Deuteronomy 18, refer to "mediums and familiar spirits" and forbid being involved with them, as they are an abomination to the Lord.

The medium was one who acted as a "go-between" to supposedly contact or communicate with the dead, but in reality they were contacting devils who convinced the mediums that they were "familiar" and could be trusted and believed. The practices associated with mediums and familiar spirits were banned in Israel, and the punishment for practicing such things was death.

Little-by-little, God started tugging at my heart. Every time I would see Sylvia or some New Age guru on TV, I changed the channel. The Holy Spirit was convicting me big time. Praise God.

6

SPIRITUAL SURGERY — CLEAN AT LAST

I couldn't get that vision of the tears in my fellow worker's eyes, out of my mind as she told me about her brother that almost ruined his life because of New Age practices. I decided I had had enough.

The next few weeks I found myself cleaning out all the filth and garbage I had been so hooked on for so many years. I threw out all the psychic and medium guru books and videos and New Age music. It was a very freeing feeling. "Neither shalt thou bring an abomination into thine house, lest thou be a cursed thing like it: but thou shalt utterly detest it, and thou shalt utterly abhor it; for it is a cursed thing," (Deuteronomy 7:26).

I started going to church. After a few months, a very sweet Christian lady approached me and talked to me for a while and then said, "The Lord has told me to talk to you today and tell you that you are playing church." She said, "I don't know exactly what that all means to you, but just pray about it and ask the Lord to reveal it to you." I was not mad at her. In fact, I thanked the lady for her obedience to the Lord that she would be so bold to tell me this.

Those words "playing church" hit me like a ton of bricks. God knew that even though I was no longer accepting New Age practices, I had in no way repented of that lifestyle or any thing I did that was not pleasing to the Lord. I was not truly sorry for my sins. It was "go on as usual."

I sat in my Lazy Boy chair in the living room and just started having a little talk with Jesus. It began with finally being totally aware and realizing that I truly was a sinner and that my good works and church traditions were nice, but they were not going to save me. I realized that I didn't have to go through someone else to get to Jesus. I went straight to Him.

I said, "Jesus, you died on the cross for me so I may be forgiven and saved. You took the beatings for me, You suffered an agonizing death and rose again for me. And how have I repaid You? By first playing games and then playing church. I am so sorry.

"I know there have been so many times that You tried to warn me, but I didn't listen. I did it my way. I am so sorry. Forgive me for all the dumb things I have done in my life. Forgive me for even so much as dabbling in New Age witchcraft. There is so much I didn't know.

"Please reveal to me, by your Holy Spirit discernment, what is real and what is not, in this world. I want you to help me clean up my life. Please help me find a church that preaches your Word.

"I want to make you not only the Saviour of my life, but the Lord of my life. I love You, Jesus, and now I know You love me. You say to come as a little child in faith, believing. I am coming to You not as a know-it-all religious person, but a person who is broken and ready to receive you as my Friend who will never leave me or forsake me. A real Friend that will tell me honestly what I am doing wrong so I can do right."

And then I started singing an old familiar child's song: "Jesus loves me, this I know, for the Bible tells me so. Little ones to Him belong. They are weak, but He is strong."

It was hard to explain what happened next, but it was like a warm blanket covered me. I remember saying "Lord it's You! It's really YOU! I realized that, had I not gotten out of that New Age witchcraft religion, there is no telling where I would be today.

I thank the Lord that he delivered me from that bondage and so much more. I just sat in the chair that night and had a long talk with Jesus about religion and New Age and all kinds of stuff from the past, and I just allowed the Lord to do some spiritual surgery on my heart. For the first time in my life I felt clean and free.

7

SPEAKING TRUTH TO DEAD RELIGION

One day I was at my mom's house and I started sharing my testimony with her. I thought she would be happy, but her comment was, "Now, please don't take this wrong but I think you have been brainwashed. When she said that, I was so hurt, but I just listened and nodded my head and listened some more. As I watched her light up another cigarette and listen to her soap operas, I thought "Who is brainwashed here?"

That afternoon some of her friends came over. We were all sitting around having some of Mom's good, homemade pie. As I took a bite, I was hearing something I had never noticed before. I was listening to an occasional swear word come out of someone's mouth. I could tell they didn't even know they were saying it. As I took another bite, I saw them all laughing at a dirty joke someone had just said.

As the afternoon progressed, I heard even more swear

words roll out referring to the price of corn and beans and the rain that they needed and were not getting.

I thought to myself. "You can swear and blame God when you don't get what you want but I have never heard you once thank God publicly for the blessings and money in the bank that you have received from that land. It's all about you and what you have and what a good farmer you are.

So again, who is brainwashed here?"

I was so mad at seeing how deceived everyone, including my Mom, really was, I decided I had to get out of there. I said a short goodbye to everyone and gave Mom a big hug and told her I loved her. While driving home I was getting madder by the minute. I thought: there really is a Devil, and like the Bible says, the Devil blinds the minds of the people so they cannot see the truth. 2 Corinthians 4:4: "In whom the god of this world hath blinded the minds of them which believe not, lest the light of the glorious gospel of Christ, who is the image of God, should shine unto them."

I turned the car around and drove to my mom's church. I prayed, "Lord give me the boldness so I can tell this pastor what you want me to tell her. I walked into the church. I knocked on the office door. The pastor opened it and welcomed me in. For a while we talked in general about Mom. She talked about how wonderful my mom was. How she enjoyed all the goodies she would give her. I nodded my head in agreement. She kept going on and on about, what I would say are, trivial things.

I finally stopped her and said, "Pastor I am very concerned about my mom. I am concerned about her spiritually." By the look on her face I could tell she didn't have a clue why I would say such a thing. She paused and said, "What do you mean? She has been baby baptized and confirmed hasn't she?"

I said, "I don't mean to be rude but Mom can be sprinkled or dunked and confirmed a hundred times, it makes no difference."

She said, "She always takes communion when she comes to church."

I said, "I am not against anyone being baptized or confirmed. But when these things are based as their ticket to heaven that's where I have a big problem. The Lord warned the Pharisees many times in the Bible about their man-made religious traditions. It's not about a religion. It's about a relationship with Jesus. It's a heart decision, not a head decision."

All of a sudden the image came to me where Jesus was so angry he was turning the tables upside down in the temple.

I told the pastor: "If she really had accepted Jesus in her heart she would not want to gossip or listen to gossip or listen to or tell dirty jokes, or watch dirty movies. If Mom was truly saved she would have a heart for the lost, unsaved people all around her. I am not talking about going to be a missionary in some other country. We need to be missionaries right here."

I could see the pastor was running out of excuses, not once opening up her Bible as she said, "Oh, your mom is a good lady. She would do anything for anybody."

Now, I felt my blood start to boil as I saw that she was really not getting it. I said, "The Lord is not tallying up how many good works we do or how self-righteous we are. The Bible says our righteousness is like filthy rags to the Lord. God is more concerned with where our heart is spiritually. I heard you ask me earlier if I knew if Mom was baptized or confirmed.

"You're asking me? If that's so important to you, then you should have concrete evidence that she is. Isn't that a requirement for communion or your church membership? Do you see how everyone just kind of takes for granted the most important decision of a person's life?"

Now, I was on a roll and remember, I was just a newly saved Christian, but getting madder by the minute as I continued, "When I told my mom I had accepted Jesus into my heart and life, my mom's comment was this, 'Judy, now don't take this wrong, but I believe you have been brainwashed.' Now you tell me who is brainwashed here. At the beginning of your church service Sunday after Sunday you read out of the front pages of a man-made book. Everyone says the same liturgy over and over.

"And then you have some more man-made liturgy and you have the congregation say the same words, 'Hear our prayer, hear our prayer.' The Lord has very strong warnings about repetitious prayers.

"And then there is communion. And, by the way, it should never have been labeled the word 'communion.' It's the Lord's Supper. When you call it communion you take the Lord out of what you are doing. But anyway, when people partake of the Lord's Supper, they are paraded up to the front like a herd of cows. After you have said the same thing to the same people over and over and over, then you tell them to 'Go in peace. Your sins are forgiven.'

"Let me ask you this. Do you really have the right to say, 'Your sins are forgiven?' Show me one verse in the Bible that says a pastor, or a clergy of any kind, has the right to proclaim your sins are forgiven."

I waited for an answer, but none came. I said, "Only the Lord Jesus can forgive a person's sins."

I could feel the anger well up inside me as I noticed that not once did Mom's pastor ever open her Bible or quote the Word of God to prove me wrong.

Which made me all the madder as I said, "You pastors are so deceived. You make people believe that the grace of God will cover you, which then gives your people the right to knowingly sin, over and over again, and not feel guilty about it. I don't know how you can sleep at night knowing that you are preaching a false gospel. I guess you just kind of skipped over that part in Galatians 1 about the false doctrine —a false gospel.

"And what's worse, when you tell people their sins are forgiven, that gives them a green light to knowingly go and sin again. But when Jesus said, 'Your sins are forgiven,' He also said, 'Now go and sin no more.' You never talk about repentance or conviction in your sermons. It's all about the blessings and love of God.

"And then you skip over the verses about Satan and devils and what they can do. And you don't give them any tools from the Word of God as to how they can fight these devils.

"Devils are real and they are not only in Africa in witch doctors. There are evil spirits everywhere. Just listen to the news and you can see them at work behind closed doors."

She didn't answer me, but, by the look on her face and the Bible verses she had, herself, read somewhere, she knew I was telling the truth.

I left there shaking I was so angry. Then tears came to my eyes and I could hardly see to drive. On the way home I passed another Lutheran Church, turned the car around and went in and said the same thing to the Lutheran pastor there as I did to Mom's pastor. He didn't open his Bible either.

He just kept looking at the open door hoping no one was listening to my conversation with him. I didn't care; I was angry at this deceptive, Lutheran religion.

As the months went on, my anger slowly turned to compassion for these deceived, religious, people. My heart was breaking. I felt I needed to do something. But where would I ever begin?

8

BURDENED IN THE LAND OF THE DECEIVED

As the months went on, the Lord started revealing things to me even more. Working as a cashier, I began to see how parents and children from many walks of life were buying things they shouldn't. Pokemon cards, Harry Potter and witchcraft books, and demonic games and toys, became something I was very concerned about.

Having been in New Age, I could see where this could lead for these children. I felt that I needed to expose this garbage, but the Devil was right there discouraging me. I would hear words like, "Who is going to listen? They are going to think that you are holier-than-thou, goody-two-shoes. Who is going to understand or care?"

Then one day a flyer came in the mail. There was a picture of Harry Potter on the front. I was almost ready to rip it into a million pieces, but instead, decided to see what it was all about. It was a seminar, at a college not far from me, about the deception in the Harry Potter books. I didn't even hesitate. I was the first one there.

The presenter was a Christian man by the name of Wendell Amstutz who is from the National Community Resource Center in Rochester, Minnesota. For 25 years Mr. Amstutz has worked with numerous police departments, courts, judges, counselors and treatment centers. He said that many people do not reject Harry Potter because they believe that Rowling's character-filled, Hogwarts' School of Witchcraft is just an imaginary place of make-believe fun. Rowling herself claims that her stories are just fantasy, but extensive research by Wendell Amstutz has demonstrated the appearance of many actual occult practices.

At the seminar, Mr. Amstutz asked all parents to please take their young children out of the room, because he was going to be reading from the Harry Potter books about things that children should not hear. There was a room that was designated just for this. After the children left he opened up the Harry Potter book and read word-for-word on page after page what really takes place in real satanic rituals. He went on to say that children are stolen and sacrificed to Satan all year long but Halloween is a holiday to these occultists and the world celebrates it like it was Christmas. In the Harry Potter Books there were not only satanic rituals but gruesome murders.

Mr. Amstutz said that these books fuel good, innocent, vulnerable teenagers to get curious and dabble in witchcraft. After seeing good kids go bad year after year, even to the extreme of getting sucked into satanic occult activity, he decided to find out how this can happen.

For years he had crisscrossed the country interviewing cult researchers, crime investigators, and taskforce members, about the occult. Unless you know the language of the occult backwards and forwards you would just think it was harmless fantasy. He said that, in the Harry Potter books, children are introduced to real witchcraft. He said that you can't tell the supposedly good, white witch from the bad, black witch because they all wear black.

And with each book they go just a little deeper. Even the media has said that these books are getting darker and darker. He said it doesn't matter if it is white witchcraft or black witchcraft it's all the same; it is very dangerous. That's why the Lord warns us in the Bible in Deuteronomy 18 not to have anything to do with it. In the seminar that lasted over 2 hours, he used the Word of God, quoting verse after verse exposing Rowling's witchcraft books.

Now, knowing even more about these books, this time from a Biblical point of view, it really grieved my spirit at my workplace every time I had to sell these awful, devilish, cards and books. It was always a big deal when the latest Harry Potter book was about to be released.

One day at work, a mother and her young son came to my cash register. The boy, who was around seven years old, wanted the latest Harry Potter book. He also had some Pokemon cards in his hands. The mother, who I could see was struggling with paying her bill, counting her dollars, said to the little boy, "We can't afford it." The boy became very angry threw away the book and the cards he had half opened. He swore at her and kicked her leg so hard that her leg buckled. He took the shopping cart and tried to tip it over. The mother paid with what money she had, and left in tears.

For some reason I felt like this was more than just a naughty child that needed a good spanking. It was much deeper and more involved than anyone knew. The boy had opened up a very dangerous door and he was hooked, but what could I say, what could I do? Even though I wanted to shout it from the rooftops: "Please don't buy these," I had to bite my lip more than once and not say anything. Well, as time went by, I put Harry Potter on the back burner, just knowing that there was nothing I could do, so why try? Nobody cared or understood.

In 1996 I met and married a wonderful man. At our wedding we asked our pastor to use: "…but as for me and my house, we will serve the LORD," (Joshua 24:15). And we asked the pastor to give the Lord's Supper and a salvation message at our wedding. Nine people gave their hearts to Jesus. To God be the glory. And the rest were either saved or walking on both sides of the fence. But good, Godly seeds were planted in everyone there that day, including my mom.

One night I got a call that my mom was dying. As I was racing to get there, I remember praying to the Lord: "Please don't let her die before she accepts You." And then the verse came to me in Romans 4:17 about calling those things as though they were even though they are not. Then my prayer turned to declaring out loud, in that car that night, that my mom will be saved, in Jesus' name. With tears streaming down my face I kept saying that over and over and over.

I said: "Devil, you can't have her; she is going to heaven. My mom will be saved in Jesus' name." When I got to my mom, she was very weak but she could say the words, "Judy, something doesn't feel right." I said, "Is it Jesus, Mom?"

And she said, "Yes." And I said, "Mom, it's okay. All you have to do is acknowledge that Jesus died for your sins and ask Him to come into your heart and forgive you. But you have to want to do this. I can't do it for you. Remember from Sunday school days the picture of Jesus knocking on the door. Remember how there is no doorknob on the outside of that door. You have to open it from the inside.

"Jesus will never force His way in. He wants you to open the door to your heart and receive Him. It's not about being baptized as a baby or confirmed. It's not about if you are good enough or even how many good or bad things you have done in your life. We have all done things we are not proud of." I said, "Mom, it's so simple and people make it so complicated with good works and manmade church traditions. It has nothing to do with good works. It's not about us and how good we are, it's about Jesus, Mom; the One that died for you and me; the One that took every sin that you and I have ever committed and cleansed our sins with the blood that He shed on the cross."

There was complete silence and then she bowed her head and closed her eyes and she gave her heart to Jesus. When she opened her eyes, with big tears, she started singing, "What a Friend we have in Jesus..." And I joined in and sang with her.

That night, right in her own home I had the honor of leading my religious, Lutheran, mom to the Lord. To God be the Glory. Even though Mom was getting weaker and weaker there was a glow on her face and peace that I had never seen before. She was taken by ambulance to the hospital and a few hours later she went to be with Jesus.

And in heaven the angels all rejoiced when a sinner repented. Luke 15:10: "Likewise, I say unto you, there is joy in the presence of the angels of God over one sinner that repenteth."

While my brother and sister and I were making funeral arrangements, I asked Mom's pastor, (the same pastor I had talked to before), if I could say a few words at her funeral. She, of course, could not say no.

At her funeral in that same Lutheran Church that she had gone to for many, many years, with a variety of religious denominations of family and friends present, I gave a testimony how Mom truly accepted the Lord Jesus Christ. To God be the Glory.

And I got "the look" on more than one face as I shared with them exactly, word-for-word, what happened. It was the same look and reaction I got when I gave my testimony in my little country Lutheran church to some religious men and women.

I had many people come up to me later and say, "That was beautiful what you said. How did you do that?" I said, "It wasn't me. It was the Lord that gave me the boldness and the peace to share this beautiful experience with you."

There were many different reactions but most were: "Oh, that's nice," and quickly changed the subject. I was hurt at their reaction. Why couldn't they be happy with me? Why were they so uncomfortable, when I was sharing with them the most important decision my mom would make in her life?

I started going to church more and my Bible of choice became several Bibles including a Women's Devotional NIV with the pretty, pink flowers on the front. Once in a while I would check out a footnote in the NIV, but for some reason they didn't seem to make any sense. It was the same feeling I got with New Age practices and my Lutheran religion in general. Something just didn't seem right. But I didn't know what.

Well, life went on as usual and so did the uneasiness I felt with certain things. This time it was about Halloween, remembering that Mr. Amstutz said that it is the Devil's holiday, the day when little children are sacrificed *in* (by) satanic cults, and the world celebrates it like it was Christmas.

One day at work, a mother, her young daughter and her teenage son came to check out at my cash register. It was October when everyone was buying Halloween junk and I was not in a good mood at all. The mother had bought black material to make a witch's costume for herself and her little girl. The little girl was screaming over and over, "I don't want to be a witch." The mother said, "You told me you wanted to be a witch. I spent all this money on this material. Now you are going to be a _____ witch!

The son wanted to buy some Halloween, demonic, blood-and-guts movies, and the evil, devilish, video game, Grand Theft Auto. The cash register prompted me to ask how old he was. He said he was 15 . I told him, "I am sorry but you cannot buy this game." Immediately his mother said "Oh for _____ sake I will buy the _____ game." The boy smiled and put his money back in his pocket. She not only bought the game and movies, she had Halloween candy, and a skeleton that said, "Don't go here," as I picked it up to scan it. She had green costume makeup and of course the little girl's black material and witch hat. Her bill came to over $75.00.

She then turned to the son and told him to take his sister, still sobbing, out to the car. Then she said to me, "I didn't want my little girl to hear this, but do you have any witch dolls? I thought that would make her feel better about being a witch for Halloween if I would buy her one of those witch dolls."

I was so frustrated and angry I told her no! She said, "You didn't even check on the doll. Are you sure?" I said in a sarcastic way: "I know we don't!" I threw the stuff in a sack as fast as I could and said abruptly, "Here!" The mother shoved the cart aside and said, "I would like to talk to your manager." I paged him and he took the lady back to his office. A little while later I saw the mother storm out of the store.

The manager called me into his office and asked me what happened. I explained and I apologized. The manager told me, "Don't do this again." As I was leaving for the day one of my fellow employees asked me if I was working on Halloween. I said "Yes."

He then asked what I was going to dress up as. He said he was going to dress up as the Devil. That is not what I needed to hear! I stared at him and snapped, "I have had a bad day. A customer really got me angry and I am going home." He put up his hands and said sarcastically: "Okay, sorry I asked."

I went home that night and got down on my knees and cried out to God: "I can't do this! I can't do what you want me to do. I am doing this all wrong. I don't know why I even bothered spending years researching and taping and recording all that stuff and spending all that money on the dangers of Harry Potter and New Age videos. Why did I bother going to that college to hear about Harry Potter. No one cares! No one understands." I was really having a pity party.

I received no great revelation from the Lord except the thought of that same verse in Philippians 3:15: "God shall reveal even this unto you." I was mad at God. I said, "And quit giving me that verse."

That night before I went to bed I was watching the 10:00

news. They were saying that Anoka, Minnesota, which is only a hundred miles from where I live, was the Halloween capital of the world. I was so mad that I quickly flipped the channel and another news story was about the latest Harry Potter book that was just about to come out at midnight.

9

SPEAKING TRUTH TO POTTERMANIA

I sat and watched all the kids that were lined up for blocks, all dressed up in their witch's costumes and round glasses and lightning bolt on their forehead. I said, "Lord, this is so sickening, seeing these parents dole out their hard-earned money literally for the Devil's glory." That night I cried myself to sleep. I couldn't even pray. The next morning I opened my eyes and tried to pray and all I could say was the word, "Jesus" and then, "Jesus, help me." And then the words started flowing and I was able to pray again. I asked the Lord to forgive me for acting so ridiculous. And then we just had a nice talk. And it was as if a black cloud left me.

I thanked the Lord for helping me. But I was still so frustrated. I kept having this feeling that I needed to do something about this Harry Potter stuff. The next day was my day off and the Lord impressed on me to go to the library to research the

Harry Potter books even further. To be honest, I really didn't want to go. I thought to myself, "No one cares or understands." But the Lord gave me no peace until I did.

I walked into the library and up to the librarian and asked her where the Harry Potter books were. She pointed over to the children's section. For some reason I took as many books as I could and then went back for more. Balancing the books in my arms I went to a table in the far corner of the library. I didn't want to be seen or bothered.

I hadn't noticed how long I had been there. I glanced at my watch. It was almost four in the afternoon. I had been there since it opened in the morning. I was just about ready to call it a day when a young lady came up to me and said, almost in an angry way, "There they are, you have them." I said, "I am sorry. Which one were you looking for?"

She was going to tell me, that is, until she took a good look at all the books, and my mountain of notes. With a puzzled look on her face she said, "Can I ask, what are you doing?" I prayed silently to myself, "Help me, Lord." I said, "I am doing some research on the Harry Potter books. She asked me why and I said, "Because I had learned that these books were somewhat questionable, and I wanted to see for myself."

Her puzzled face turned to anger. She said. "Oh! Everyone thinks these books are questionable, but they are okay." I froze and just looked at her with a concerned look on my face while continuing to ask for the Lord's guidance.

She then asked: "What is so wrong with them?"

I said, "This is what concerns me. In the story is this character who whines and cries and moans a lot. In fact her name is Moaning Myrtle. She is teased and put down and she feels so bad about herself, she tries to kill herself."

She said with disgust, "Where does it say that in the book?"

I looked at my notes where I had scribbled the words, "suicide: Chamber of Secrets, page 156 -157. I said, "Harry and his friends have just entered the girl's bathroom where Myrtle says:

"My life was nothing but misery at this place and now people come along ruining my death!"

"We wanted to ask you if you've seen anything funny lately," said Hermione quickly, because a cat was attacked right outside your front door on Halloween."

"Did you see anyone near here that night?" said Harry.

"I wasn't paying attention," said Myrtle dramatically. "Peeves upset me so much I came in here and tried to *kill* myself. Then, of course, I remembered that I'm...I'm..."

"Already dead," said Ron helpfully.

Myrtle gave a tragic sob, rose up in the air, turned over, dived head first into the toilet, splashing water all over them and vanishing from sight, although from the direction of her muffled sobs, she had come to rest somewhere in the U-bend.

Harry and Ron stood with their mouths open, but Hermione shrugged wearily and said, "Honestly, that was almost cheerful for Myrtle. Come on, let's go."

After I showed her what it really said, word for word, I waited for a response. She looked shocked. She said "I had no idea. I read that book, Chamber of Secrets from cover to cover and I guess I never saw that."

I told her I couldn't believe that someone could write a children's book portraying suicide as okay and being almost cheerful. Like it's no big deal. Suicide is an awful thing. And

Rowling makes light of such an awful and tragic thing, almost to the point of glamorizing it!

I told her that my first husband had committed suicide. Needless to say these books are a very sore subject with me.

She asked me what else was in these books. I told her about the seminar I had gone to at a college exposing the Harry Potter books. The presenter had done extensive research on children in cults. He couldn't say enough about how dangerous these books really are. I said, "When I first learned this, I wanted to take every Harry Potter book and tear it to shreds. I was so angry at how this Rowling has deceived, bewitched, and manipulated the world into thinking that these books are moral, okay, fun, fantasy, and harmless children's books. Rowling said herself in an SSC interview, October 17, 1999, '**I think they're very moral books.**'

"How can they be moral books when children of all ages are reading about satanic rituals, the drinking of animal blood, the way drugs were glorified, and that you're what the potion's teacher refers to as a 'dunderhead' if you don't know how to make drugs? How can they be moral books when Harry and his friends lie and cheat?

"And if that isn't sickening enough, children of all ages can read in the books and hear on the big movie screen, swear words now and then. How can they be moral books when there are too-many-to-mention gruesome murders and people tortured, and in one verse, killing is done for fun? How can she say these are moral books when an object that is called a mandrake plant, when pulled out of dirt on the big screen, looks like a real, crying, screaming baby that gets cut up, stewed and eaten? What would have ever possessed this J.K. Rowling to write such horrible storyline?"

She said that she had no idea that all these awful things were in these books. She said she had read every book from cover to cover and went to several Harry Potter movies and never once saw it like this. She said that she had come to the library that day because she was looking for a certain Harry Potter book that her son wanted. He happened to be home from school sick that day.

I asked her if she had ever heard of the fact that the composition of rat poison is approximately 98% harmless (and edible) corn meal, but 2% strychnine that does the job!

I said, "I know you are a good mother and you care about your children. You mentioned that your son was sick. You would never hide poison in his medicine and tell him this will make you feel better." She said "Of course not, and you have helped me realize that."

I said, "I cannot take any of the credit. I give all the glory to God for opening up my eyes about this."

With tears in her eyes she couldn't thank me enough for telling her about the books.

She said, "I have seen you some place," and I told her where I worked. She thanked me and left. A few days later a lady approached me at work and said to me, "I can't thank you enough." I was shocked. I said, "What do you mean?" She said, "That young lady that you talked to in the library is my daughter. I have been trying to tell her about these awful books for years.

Again I said, "I cannot take any of the credit. I give all the glory to God. That was a divine appointment." She said, "I know what you mean and I can't thank you enough for being obedient to the Lord's calling." I went home that day so blessed and thanked the Lord many times. I was glad that I listened to the Lord's prompting to go that day.

So, at this point, let's switch on our imagination again and visit Harry Potter from Satan's perspective.

10

HARRY POTTER AND SATAN'S ROTTEN APPLE CART

As we look in again on Satan, he is holding court, reviewing the success of one of his more accomplished accomplices.

A proud devil paraded up to the front with a rotten apple cart full of paperbacks and some very thick, hard-cover books, and said, "Well, this is how I did it. Years ago I got this lady on welfare, which took some doing, but I got the job done. Then I gave her 'one little thought' which led to another and another and another which led to the —drum roll please— the Harry Potter books. Her name is J.K. Rowling. Now mind you, I could have never convinced her to do this if she was one of those Holy-Spirit-discerning Christians."

You could hear Satan's devils screech with fear and anger as Satan growled in disgust, "I hate those kinds of Christians. If she would have been one of those Christians she would have known immediately where the thoughts were coming from and rebuked that evil thought in a heartbeat!"

"Thanks to me," the devil continued, "That didn't happen and I must say she has been a real trooper, listening to me tell her what to write.

"So now, with that in mind, let me tell you a little bit about her books. Her first book, or should I say *my* first book, Harry Potter and the Sorcerer's Stone, deals with Harry's parents being murdered. Harry had to go live with what Rowling portrayed as a dull, boring, stupid family. But one day Harry is magically transported out of this dull, boring, stupid, family, into the exciting life of witchcraft and wizardry.

"And get this guys: In my first book, Sorcerer's Stone, on page 58, let me read to you what the end results of this Harry Potter guy will be: 'Seven years there and he won't know himself. He will be with youngsters of his own sort, for a change, and he'll be under the greatest headmaster….'[2]

"Isn't that just so cool? He won't know himself. Well, continuing on, Harry quickly learns that people, like his family back home, are not who you want to be like or around. Rowling refers to them as muggles. These muggles also don't want to have anything to do with witchcraft. I had Rowling refer to these kinds of people, these muggles in the book, as inferior, less intelligent, and slow to catch on to truth; stupid, ugly, boring, and are not worthy of living. Rowling herself said in an interview that these muggles are 'not completely stupid' (Associated Press, July 6, 2000).

---

2) Rowling, J.K. (2012-03-27). Harry Potter and the Sorcerer's Stone (Book 1) (Kindle Locations 1042-1043). Pottermore Limited. Kindle Edition.

"On the other hand, witches are portrayed as friendly, helpful, positive, supportive, good, exciting, and powerful! I made sure that these muggles, these ordinary people, are so hated that there are characters who torture and murder them. In fact in one book, killing is done for fun. There are descriptive murders galore in these books. And, yes, even the granddaddy of them all, suicide, is addressed in this book and, I might add, not in an educational, but almost cheerful kind of way."

"Suicide!" Satan shouted with excitement. "Tell me more, tell me more!"

The devil was rummaging through all the books, "Ah, here it is, Harry Potter and the Chamber of Secrets. In this book I actually put a bug in Rowling's ear to create a girl by the name of Moaning Myrtle, who thinks she is fat, ugly, miserable, moping, and pimply."

Satan said, with excitement in his voice, "Lots of children feel that way at some time in their lives. We make sure of that! So, here is where we get the reader hooked on thinking, 'Oh, that's me. Rowling is so caring to think of me, too. I have felt like that.'"

"Now, here's the good part," the devil continues. "Once Rowling has their attention, the reader can be manipulated in any way, shape, or form.

"In fact in Harry Potter and the Goblet of Fire, on page 676, I popped 'one little thought' in Rowling's mind to place in the book: 'Decent people are so easy to manipulate.'

"So now, continuing with this wonderful saga, this Moaning Myrtle character is teased by many. In fact, many talk about her behind her back and not in a nice way. So what does she do? Well, she feels so miserable and hopeless, she tries to kill herself, but then she realizes she is already dead."

"You are such a genius." Satan shouted. "Tell us more!"

The devil went on to say, "I not only inspire Rowling to talk about and portray taking one's own life as being no biggy, but to make it even more acceptable, I had Rowling plant a seed in the subconscious mind of the reader that suicide is even an honorable way to help others.

"So I had Rowling create these two characters, Nicolas Flamel and his wife Perenelle. They are going to do the honorable thing and kill themselves to hide the secret of the Philosopher's Stone. But does that concern them? No way, because Nicolas has found a way for them both to live on and on and on and on. It's called the Elixir of Life."

Satan rubbed his hands together and shouted, "Now isn't this suicide and murder and reincarnation circle-of-life stuff just a peachy-keen lesson we are injecting subconsciously into the children's minds? I can't wait to hear what happens next."

With a prideful look the devil continued, "In Harry Potter and the Sorcerer's Stone we pick it up on page 297:

Harry has just been told what Nicolas and his wife are going to do. Harry says, 'But that means he and his wife will die, won't they?' 'They have enough Elixir stored to set their affairs in order and then, yes, they will die.' Dumbledore smiled at the look of amazement on Harry's face. 'To one as young as you, I'm sure it seems incredible, but to Nicolas and Perenelle, it really is like going to bed after a very, very long day. After all, to the well-organized mind, death is but the next great adventure.'

"And then on page 302, I have Rowling repeat the same statement so the reader is sure to get it in their subconscious mind, that death by suicide or any way is just fine. There Rowling writes again: 'To the well-organized mind, death is but the next great adventure.'"

Satan growled in anger, "That is true if they are really, truly saved and know they will be in heaven with Jesus when they die, like it says in the Bible in 2 Corinthians 5. We surely don't want that truth plastered all over the book. The truth that will make them free, (John 8:32). Mum's the word about that. So let's drop that little tidbit of information. I want to hear more about this reincarnation, deception, and the afterlife."

"Oh, yes! The afterlife. That's right down my alley!" The devil of reincarnation said. "That's where I make people believe they don't really, physically die, they live on and on and on and on as someone else. They believe that, when a person dies, their spirit goes into the great Reincarnation Cycle, to await the next body into which they can begin again and start the 'next great adventure.' This is exactly the doctrine of death that we want children to learn about."

With a big, mischievous grin the devil laughed, "But you know, it's funny, how, in their past life, they were never one of my drunk drivers that was killed or better yet who killed someone on the highway. They were never a homeless person living under a bridge. In their past life they were always a famous person, like a queen or king or president or somebody like that.

"The reincarnation thing fits very well with New Agers indoctrinating unsuspecting, vulnerable people. Kinda what we so cleverly convinced New Age gurus to believe and are telling everyone about. We even have some planted on TV talk shows. So it doesn't matter who dies or how they die. When we put that "one little thought" in a child's or even an adult's mind, to go and blow someone's brains out, they don't feel guilty about doing it. They may even think they are doing them a favor."

Satan said with a big, ugly, vindictive smile on his face: "That makes suicide or murdering someone perfectly okay. This is straight from our wonderful, deceptive, pagan witchcraft, new age philosophy."

The devil continued: "'If it feels right, do it' is being taught to the children through the Harry Potter books, and believe me, they are taking it all in. So, by getting the message you can live on and on and on in another life, suicide or even murder is a piece of cake."

The devil got a sparkle in his eye as he went on to say, "Oh, yes! And speaking of our suicide and death education, there are many vivid explanations of people being tortured and murdered all over the books. Too many to even mention. But the children or readers of all ages get a taste of it big time.

"And if this isn't the cat's meow, we have children reading about someone torturing and killing a cat. And Harry and his friends see the cat hanging by its tail. There is a puddle of blood on the floor. And if that isn't wonderfully gruesome enough, we have baby-like creatures that are pulled out of the ground. And when they are older they are cut up and put in a stew and eaten.

"We find this happening in the Chamber of Secrets. In Hogwarts School of Wizardry, Harry and his classmates are in what Rowling calls Herbology Class. The teacher, Professor Sprout, is telling Harry and classmates to put on some earmuffs and to make sure their ears are completely covered because the cry of the Mandrake is fatal to anyone who hears it.

"In the movie, The Chamber of Secrets, these mandrakes look a whole lot like real babies and make an extremely long, loud, piercing, shrieking scream that may just very well hurt the movie goers hearing without them ever knowing it."

"The more kids of any age lose their hearing because of loud music or anything, is music to my ears," Satan said with a smile. "But do we care? I hardly think so!"

"Anyway," says the devil, "Continuing in Chamber of Secrets on page 93 and 94, Rowling writes:

Instead of roots, a small, muddy, and extremely ugly baby popped out of the Earth. The leaves were growing right out of his head. He had pale green, mottled skin, and was clearly bawling at the top of his lungs. Professor Sprout took a large plant pot from under the table and plunged the Mandrake into it, burying him in dark, damp, compost, only the tufted leaves were visible.

Professor Sprout dusted off her hands, gave them all a thumbs-up, and removed her own ear muffs. "As our Mandrakes are only seedlings, their cries won't kill, yet," she said calmly as though she'd just done nothing more exciting than water a begonia. "However, they will knock you out for several hours, and as I'm sure none of you want to miss your first day back. Make sure your ear muffs are securely in place while you work."

"Rowling goes on with the fact that the Mandrakes didn't like coming out of the earth, but didn't seem to want to go back into it either: 'They squirmed, kicked, flailed their sharp little fists, and gnashed their teeth. Harry spent ten whole minutes trying to squash a particularly fat one into a pot.'

"Notice I had Rowling write the word 'baby.' Not a plant,

but a baby popped out of the earth that squirmed, kicked, flailed his sharp little fists. I love it!

"On the big movie screen this is a fully-formed human baby in every respect, with the one minor exception that the trunk and leaves of the Mandrake were coming straight out of the top of the baby's head. The baby is shades of green and even some bluish purple. Maybe that's a sign that it may be dying. Rowling loves to write about anything to do with people being tortured and death and dying. And, without the Holy Spirit's conviction in her to tell her this is wrong, we can continue to work on her mind.

"Professor Sprout goes on to say, 'Four to a tray —there is a large supply of pots here —compost in the sacks over there— and be careful of the Venomous Tentacula! It's teething.'"

Satan said, "Oh baby, baby! This is getting better all the time! Now the baby mandrake is teething? Teething like a real, live baby! This gets better all the time!"

The devil went on to say, "Now even though the reader knows that this is not a real human baby, even though they certainly look like fully formed human babies, they are presented as not human, but only the root system of the Mandrake plant. Which reminds me of our wonderful abortion rights where a young, scared, teenage mom is reminded that it's not a real human but only tissue matter, a blob of flesh —a fetus. And to the extreme, some babies are being raised in our satanic covens simply to be sacrificed, a practice done on Halloween."

Satan said, "Oh! Did you say Halloween? That's my special day! The day children are sacrificed to me. Parents have no idea they are glorifying my special day by dressing their little ones up like witches and goblins, and Dracula and blood-and-guts costumes. I love it when I see children and adult Halloween parties with eyeballs floating in a bloody, red-colored punch —and cookie-dough fingers and…and…"

The devil interrupted, "Hey, I don't mean to be rude. But I need to get on with my presentation. We could all go on for hours and hours sharing what we have seen on Halloween. It's so wonderful. But let's get back to what's really going on in these Harry Potter books. Parents have no idea that we are introducing them to real witchcraft 101. And we can tell that they are hooked, because they can't wait for the next book to come out. It's almost like for moments in time they are hypnotized into another world. They don't know it's our world!

"So now, getting back to the demonic meanings in the Chamber of Secrets, as the storyline returns to the Mandrake plant, there is a very interesting little fact that I am not only talking about murdering babies, but fully grown people! Continuing in the Chamber of Secrets, on page 234, we put that 'one little thought' into the reader's subconscious mind that mandrakes are almost human beings as they read:

…Madam Pomfrey was pleased to report that the Mandrakes were becoming moody and secretive, meaning that they were fast leaving childhood. 'The moment their acne clears up, they'll be ready for repotting again,' Harry heard her telling Filch kindly one afternoon. 'And after that, it won't be long until we're cutting them up and stewing them. You'll have Mrs. Norris [petrified cat] back in no time.'

"And a little further into the same book the reader's subconscious mind is reinforced with that 'one little thought' that they really are human beings and not just a plant as we see on page 251:

…in March several of the Mandrakes threw a loud and raucous party in greenhouse three. This made Professor Sprout very happy. 'The moment they start trying to move into each other's pots, we'll know they're fully mature,' she told Harry'

"Abortion, like human sacrifice, is very necessary to Hogwarts School of Witchcraft and Wizardry, whether a whole bunch of these mandrake babies are cut up and stewed in a pot and eaten or 50 million unborn babies are mutilated and killed."

Satan said with a smile on his face, "To a young reader growing up with these books, this makes our act of abortion in real life look more acceptable and better and better all the time. You don't have to treat it with respect because it's just a 'blob of flesh.' It's not a real, living, breathing baby.

"And speaking of abortion it's always good to make a person who has had an abortion feel real bad all their lives, when *they just need to surrender their lives to Jesus and ask Him to forgive them* and they will know in their hearts that they would never have the desire to want to do anything like that again. But keep that quiet! We wouldn't want anyone to know that. Mum's the word."

The devil went on to say, "So not only do we have killings for fun and suicide being cheerful and abortion perfectly okay, we also have children reading about satanic rituals."

Satan said, "Oh! This is too much. Are you talking about what really goes on in a real satanic ritual? The devil said, "You got it boss! I slipped it in on page 256 of Harry Potter and the Sorcerer's Stone:

"'Then, out of the shadows, a hooded figure came crawling across the ground like some stalking beast. Harry, Malfoy, and

Fang stood transfixed. The cloaked figure reached the unicorn, lowered its head over the wound in the animal's side, and began to drink its blood.'

"But the fun doesn't stop there. In that same book, Harry Potter and the Sorcerer's Stone, we have Harry and his friends and classmates in drug-making class or, as I like to call it, potions class, learning how to make drugs. Rowling refers to some of the drugs with the cutesy name 'polyjuice.'"

The devil went on to say, "Now let me make this very clear. Like suicide and baby killing, the drug message is not that drugs are bad —stay far away; just say no— but the message in these Harry Potter books is: you had better learn how to make drugs and take drugs in just the right way or else you will be labeled a dunderhead. And you will never succeed.

"Let me read what the potions teacher, Professor Snape, is saying to Harry and his friends and classmates as we pick it up on Page 137 of Harry Potter and the Sorcerer's Stone:

'As there is little foolish wand-waving here, many of you will hardly believe this is magic. I don't expect you will really understand the beauty of the softly simmering cauldron with its shimmering fumes, the delicate power of liquids that creep through human veins, bewitching the mind, ensnaring the senses…. I can teach you how to bottle fame, brew glory, even stopper death —if you aren't as big a bunch of dunderheads as I usually have to teach.'

More silence followed this little speech. Harry and Ron exchanged looks with raised eyebrows. Hermione Granger was on the edge of her seat and looked desperate to start proving that she wasn't a dunderhead.

'Potter!' said Snape suddenly. 'What would I get if I added

powdered root of asphodel to an infusion of wormwood?'

Satan said, "Hey guys, these are real drugs that were banned in some countries. And did you notice the words 'stopper death?' That's all about living on and on and on and on when you die. It's the New Ager's reincarnation circle of life again. I love it!"

The devil continues: "And may I emphasize the accurate way that I inspire Rowling to describe these drugs or *potions* like she calls them. How inviting drugs are on the human senses: '...creeping through human veins... bewitching the mind... ensnaring the senses.'"

"You can hardly get a better description of potion making, drug use, and drug glorification than this! Don't you just love it?

"And of course I would never have Harry and his friends say that drugs are bad for you. Instead, it is the thing to do. This is straight from our pagan-witchcraft-New-Age philosophy: 'If it feels right, do it!' is being taught to the children through the Harry Potter books, and believe me, they are taking it all in.

"And did you notice the word *dunderhead*, and how Rowling had Hermione, Harry's friend, wanting to get this drug potion right so she would not be labeled a dunderhead? That's someone who is too dumb to learn. So, believe me, you don't want to be labeled a dunderhead so you better pay attention to the teacher and learn how to make these drug potions.

"Of course I can't have the drug-making class too serious, so a few pages later I keep the reader entertained with a somewhat humorous side of making drugs. The class was learning how to make a potion to cure boils. And a kind of nerdy student by the name of Neville mixed the potion wrong and it burned holes in people's shoes. Within seconds the whole class was standing on their stools while Neville, who was drenched in the potion, moaned in pain as angry red boils sprang up all over his arms and legs. He was definitely classified as a dunderhead or what the teacher then referred to him as an 'idiot boy.'"

Satan said, "Idiot boy and dunderhead and, —oh yes, muggles. I love those wonderful negative words. They are beautiful music to my ears!"

The devil said, "Now what you are about to learn next seems quite innocent in the book, the Prisoner of Azkaban. Rowling has a cute little candy shop called Honeydukes. In this candy shop are jelly slugs, chocolate frogs, ice mice that squeak when you eat them, and guess what else is in this cute little candy shop: None other than acid pops that burn holes in your tongue. How about burning holes in your brain? How many people do we have hooked on the real street drug, acid, and we got Rowling portraying this dangerous drug like a piece of candy. I love it!"

Satan said, "Oh! tell me more!"

The devil continued, "Not only is acid pops sold in the Honeydukes candy store, there is something Rowling refers to as BLOOD POPS! So, just where did the blood come from? Which animal or even child had to be sacrificed on Halloween for a blood lollipop?

"I made sure that there is a persistent fascination with blood in the Potter books that is downplayed in the movies so that it doesn't gross out unsuspecting parents. In the books, limbs are severed in rituals, there is the drinking of blood from a dead animal, and Harry's 'shed blood' allows evil Lord Voldemort to rise from the dead which is a real mocking of the resurrection of Jesus Christ!"

Satan and his cohorts all cheered and laughed as the devil continued: "In Harry Potter and the Sorcerer's Stone, children of all ages can read what happens in our real, satanic blood rituals: 'The cloaked figure reached the unicorn, lowered its head over the wound in the animal's side and began to drink its blood.' And then, what's even better, they can see it on the big movie screen. It's so touching it almost makes me cry real drops of blood."

Satan said, "And no one knows they are reading about real, satanic rituals. How positively, wonderfully sick! Certainly no parent or school official in their right mind would want these ideas in the minds of their children. Drugs, or polyjuice potion, like the clever, cutesy name Rowling uses, have always been a large part of our witchcraft and sorcery. The drugs are used to induce altered states of consciousness and to enhance the person's ability to communicate with the spirit world."

Satan smiled, "Oh! The spirit world. I love it. People think of the spirit world as friendly ghosts, Casper-the-friendly-ghost-type ghosts. Little do they know that ghosts are demonic spirits, masquerading as their dead relatives. They are called familiar spirits and God said to have nothing to do with them. There are people that go ghost hunting for a living and have no idea how dangerous this is."

"Speaking of ghosts," continued the devil, "In the movie, Harry Potter and Goblet of Fire, Harry has just entered the bathroom as Moaning Myrtle the ghost says, 'Oh, hello Harry. Long time no see. Hmm, I was circling a blocked drain the other day and I swear I saw some polyjuice potion. Not being a bad boy again, are you, Harry? I'd put it in the water if I were you.' In other words, you better not get caught with drugs in school, but if you do, have a plan to cover it all up.

"Also in the movie, Goblet of Fire, we have Moaning Myrtle saying to Harry,

Nobody missed me even when I was alive. Took them hours to find my body —I know, I was sitting there waiting for them. Olive Hornby came into the bathroom. 'Are you in here again, sulking Myrtle?' she said, 'Because Professor Dippet asked me to look for you.' And then she saw my body... Ooooh, she didn't forget that until her dying day, I made sure of that....

"In our Harry Potter books we not only have death and suicide and abortion and drug education, but we also have Ron and his friends and characters in the books lying and cheating and the teachers most of the time let them do it.

"Rowling laughs at the complaints, declaring: 'I am not trying to influence anyone into black magic. That's the very last thing I'd want to do. My wizarding world is a world of the imagination. I think it's a moral world,' says Rowling, quoted in USA Week, and online, November 14, 1999. Rowling says that it really does not matter what books children look at. Let them read anything they want, is her position: 'I think they're very moral books.' (Rowling, SSC interview, October 17, 1999.)"

Satan shouted, "Did you hear it? She said herself they are moral books. Boy have we got her where we want her. In these so-called good, moral books for sweet, little, innocent children, Harry and his friends and some other characters not only dabble in real witchcraft, cheat on exams, lie up a storm, but they also spew out swear words here and there just to keep things interesting. And if they are too young to read, they can hear the swear words in a CD, on a DVD, or better yet, on the big movie screen. How wonderful is that?"

"Harry Potter is only a story," Satan laughed. "A fairy tale that is supposedly harmless for children to read. If anyone would bother to check these books out literally, or make the time to study them deeper, they would clearly see that it makes the occult look trivial, and that it is a sneaky way of us introducing and promoting the occult among children. Children are no dummies. They know full well that the story is make-believe.

"But on the subconscious level, they have absorbed it as experience, and this experience tells all those Curious Georges at a boring drug or drinking party that it's okay to dabble in some witchcraft stuff. If Harry Potter can do it they sure can. They just know it is harmless fun to kinda liven up the party, even though we know different. These books are not enlightening; they are taking them deeper and deeper into darkness and no one is the wiser!

"Listen to this. I love it! *Time*, in partnership with CNN, Sunday, Oct. 27, 2002, By Jess Cagle: 'The new film's scarier tone is true to the books —and aimed at an older audience. The first film was funny; this is even funnier. The first film had action. This has even more. It is also much scarier. Like Rowling's books, the movies are *becoming darker* and more intense as they progress.'

"Now mind you," said the devil, "I do throw in some humor and some morality here and there —just to keep some so-called Christians endorsing the books; so church parents can allow their children to read them with no problem. And if these books are being endorsed by so-called Christians, then the sky's the limit for any parent to let their children read the books. But I make sure that these books get progressively darker and darker.

"These images that are brought to especially young children's minds are wonderful. But it's funny how some parents would never allow their young children to watch a gory blood-and-guts movie like Friday the 13th on Halloween, but they pay good money to see their children entertained by real, satanic, rituals, blood-and-guts, and swearing, in a movie theatre. I love it! The more the merrier, I say. Like I said earlier, and I know you won't mind me repeating what Rowling says in an SSC interview, October 17, 1999: 'I think they're very moral books.'"

Satan said, "You know, looking back at the Columbine School shooting in Colorado and the Virginia Tech shooting it was remembered for a while and then, because it didn't hit home personally, in time, they forget about it and life goes on —until we help to make the next real-life horror story. Like one newscaster I heard on TV one day say, after the Virginia Tech shooting 'This is truly a dark day and if you think it isn't going to get even *darker* you have your head in the sand.' The key word and the word we really need to pay close attention to is the word *dark*. This is just the tip of the iceberg. This *darkness* is spreading fast and no one is the wiser.

"You know, I really need to say this, but way back when the western world was relatively free from the occult, hidden, *dark*, madness, you knew who the good guy was because he had the white hat and white horse. And the bad guy had the black hat and black horse. That was a given.

"But with the Harry Potter books you don't know the bad witches from the good guys because they all wear black. Now today, thanks to TV, movies, music, and occult books, the safety zone people have long taken for granted is fading away. Children are all innocent, curious, vulnerable people and, sometimes, innocent dabbling in the seemingly exciting unknown is enticing to any child. I am happy to say it's like playing Russian roulette with the mind and soul.

"As a culture, people, or muggles as I like to call them, are getting over the shock of what is the dark side. Thanks to books and movies and TV that glorify the seemingly innocent occult, we are slowly getting them desensitized to it.

"Unless someone knows our New Age, occult teachings backward and forward, they will be inclined to think it's just another innocent fantasy movie or TV show, video game, or book. We can sneak in a video game that glorifies raping and murdering and being disrespectful to law enforcement like Grand Theft Auto, and TV shows that make witches and spells look like the everyday norm."

The devil went on to say, "Although we have packaged these Harry Potter books in fantasy and written them in humorous and entertaining terms, avid young readers are fed a steady diet of true, occult disciplines, some overt and others more subtle. But all, nevertheless, include supernatural concepts that the Bible warns against being involved in.

"Throughout the books, Harry learns and practices dark skills forbidden by the Creator God of the Bible, such as sorcery, astrology, spell casting, necromancy, and divination to name a few. Furthermore, these books glorify Harry's participation in unbiblical values.

"Like I said before, Harry steals, lies, cheats, is rude, rebellious, and even breaks 'wizardry' rules which he not only gets away with, but is often rewarded for by his occult teachers."

If Harry Potter is so innocent, as some suggest, then why would the *London Sunday Times*, July 12, 2000 edition, liken Potter to Aleister Crowley's satanism? Crowley is considered one of the most evil men ever to have lived. Why would horror novelist Stephen King write in the *New York Times*, July 23, 2000, that Potter would provide children with a good introduction to his own gruesome and devilish horror novels? A high priest of the First Church of Satan in Salem, Massachusetts, in a July 2000 edition of *Time* magazine said that they have had more applicants than they can handle, thanks to Harry Potter!

All of this just confirms that Harry Potter is a book series and film that is morally flawed, filled with egocentric characters who lie, cheat, steal, use profanity, spill blood, refuse to repent, and practice occult techniques. Harry is portrayed as the character that uses "good evil" to overcome "bad evil." In the end, it's all about evil!

"It's just fantasy, you say?" When did God say that real life must be holy, but the fantasy we read or watch can be occultic? We're to "abstain from all appearance of evil" (1 Thessalonians 5:22). It is clear from James 4:7-8 and 2 Timothy 2:22 that we are to flee evil and cling to good. It's my opinion that Harry Potter is one of the most blatant examples of "evil called good" (Isaiah 5:20) in the 21st century.

Let's check back in on the devil's report: "J.K. Rowling has stated that she intended for her Harry Potter books to be read by children approximately ages 10 and up. (The books are wildly popular among children as young as age 6 or 7). Rowling has done her homework and has really convinced, or better said, bewitched the world into thinking that these books are, like she said herself, 'very moral books.'

"In the Chamber of Secrets one of the most wonderful, horrifying images is how sweet, 11-yr-old Ginny Weasley, the younger sister of Harry's best friend, Ron, is dying. Tom Riddle, who is really Lord Voldemort, feeds off of her energy, growing stronger on 'a diet of her deepest fears, her darkest secrets.' She eventually comes to the point that she was controlled enough by Voldemort to kill animals and loose the terrible Serpent of Slytherin on four children. This conjures up a frightening picture of a young child killing animals and attempting to kill people because she was somehow *taken over* by Voldemort."

Satan said, "Taken over, that's what we love to do. Take over peoples' lives without them even knowing it, and what makes it so easy is they don't believe demon powers exist. This is great. This imagery of suicide and drugs and murders, and more murders, is just what we want, especially for young children to get in their little minds. We want to take them over big time.

"And then a naïve, undiscerning parent might say that they had books on witches when they were growing up. To that I say: but those books were not showing someone how to actually dabble in our real occult witchcraft. Those old books did provide introduction to witches, like for instance, where the witch wanted to kill Hansel and Gretel but the children ran away and got out of the witch's forest as fast as they could. But then in later years I took it one step further and made —The Wizard of Oz.

"Don't tell anyone but there really is a hidden message to learn from the old classic movie, The Wizard of Oz. I started out with a good message with Dorothy and the tin man and scarecrow and cowardly lion, but what I also did in that movie was introduce the world to the good witch and the bad witch and of course the wizard of Oz and no one is wiser than he. Get it? *Wizard*, of Oz?

"In fact, it became a classic. I love it. The wicked witch with her ugly green face saying to Dorothy 'I'll get you my pretty!!!!!!!!!!!' In other words I'll get you, little girl or boy. I'll get you, vulnerable, curious teenager. And that's exactly what is happening through the tools like the Harry Potter books.

"It's the good ole rotten apples all over again. Evil is good and good is evil. The 'good' witches practice 'white magic', while the bad witches practice the 'dark arts.' Readers become fascinated with the *magic* used which we are sure to explain in remarkable detail. I guess they just don't know or care that *God* is clear in *Scripture* that even choosing to read books on witchcraft is wrong, let alone any practice of magic. It's all an *abomination* to him. God doesn't distinguish between white and dark *magic* since they both originate from the same source."

The devil continued: "It's great that not many people read about our devices in Deuteronomy 18:10-14 anymore:

"There shall not be found among you any one that maketh his son or his daughter to pass through the fire, or that useth divination, or an observer of times, or an enchanter, or a witch, or a charmer, or a consulter with familiar spirits, or a wizard, or a necromancer.

For all that do these things are an abomination unto the Lord: and because of these abominations the Lord thy God doth drive them out from before thee. Thou shalt be perfect with the Lord thy God. For these nations, which thou shalt possess, hearkened unto observers of times, and unto diviners: but as for thee, the Lord thy God hath not suffered thee so to do."

"Only a few believe that all witches are evil. I have good witches that want nothing to do with evil or do satanic rituals —they just worship mother earth and creation and who knows what else. But what they don't realize is, that if they *are not* following the Lord Jesus Christ with their whole heart, mind, body, and soul 24/7, guess who they are being controlled by 24/7. I love it.

"So this is how we laid the ground work for the present-day Harry Potter books with more good and bad witches. I also made sure there are elements of fantasy and good story-telling in these books. At the same time, the whole story is set in an occult context, and with references to real occult practices and viewpoints mixed in with fantasy. The idea of using sorcery to fight evil, or using good witchcraft to fight bad, is a major component of the plot.

"There is a difference between fantasy and the occult. Fantasy can be used in a way that totally leaves out references to the occult. But this is not what happens in my books. Instead, fantasy feeds on the occult and is fueled by it. Yes, this is just a story, but stories can teach and influence. Stories can present ideas and endorse worldviews. Does this book desensitize children to the occult? What happens when they get older and encounter peers who practice white or black magic, cast spells, and attempt spirit contact? They are all set to go.

"These practices have become more popular, and are already

widespread among adolescents. I made sure that Harry's witchy friends are made to appear very wise and powerful next to his boring, know-nothing, average, 'muggle' family members. Harry Potter is only a story, a fairy tale that is supposedly harmless for children to read. But as you can see, I have made the occult look trivial, and that is a sneaky way of promoting page after page and book after book of sugar-coated poison. Children know full well that the story is make-believe. But on the subconscious level, they have absorbed it as experience, which feeds their curiosity for the mysterious, forbidden unknown which is highly enticing to check out.

"The author herself admits this, in an interview by *Stories from the Web*. When asked if she had 'any clues about the next book,' her answer was clear: 'I don't want to give anything away, but I can tell you that the books are getting *darker!*' Again, on CBS *The Early Show*, New York, March 7, 2006, a quote from Daniel Radcliffe, who plays Harry Potter in the movie, Goblet of Fire, said, 'It's very intense, it's very *dark*. We sort of say every year that the films are getting *darker*, and I think they absolutely do, but I think we've gone even further to the *darkness* in this film.'

"This is just a glimpse into the world of the *dark side* of Harry Potter: loyal friend, expert athlete, boy wizard. For today's young readers, Harry Potter has become something of a hero and 'my kids are reading' says the parents. Harry is portrayed with enough charisma to force even a nonreader to turn off the TV, or put down the joystick, open a book, tear through over 700 pages and stand in line at midnight and wait with much anticipation for more.

"It is a wonderful, *dark* day in the neighborhood for me,"

laughs the devil, "when I will again see little children with their lightning-bolt tattoo pasted on their forehead and their black-rimmed, Harry Potter glasses on, dressed up like little wizards and witches, waiting patiently for the latest book.

"In fact I have Rowling direct her publisher how these books are to be released down to the minute to: what else — the bewitching hour: midnight! What are little children doing there, so long past their bed times? Does Rowling really care about children? No way! And notice, too, that Harry comes back for more and more as each book takes him deeper and deeper into witchcraft.

"And from there our friend, our pal, J.K. Rowling, opened up a boatload of Pandora boxes with so-called good and bad witches shows on TV, etc. I love it. Now we have curious, naïve, teenagers dabbling into dangerous witchcraft. And now the blood-sucking Vampire books and movies and the seductive, heart-stopping, love story of the Twilight Series, are the frozen, coldly-calculated icing on the bloody, rotten apple cake."

Satan said, "Hey! I just thought of something. With the satanic ritual of drinking of blood in the Harry Potter series and now the blood-sucking Vampire Series, we are mocking the most sacred issue to those Christians —their precious message of the shed blood of the Lord Jesus Christ. Oh, isn't that just too, too bad."

One of the devils said, "And then I hear people say, 'Well, I just read the books. I stay away from witches.' I guess it just kind of slipped their minds what the Lord said in 1 Thessalonians 5:22: 'Abstain from all appearance of evil.' In fact, there are lots more scriptures I hope they forget:

"Were they ASHAMED when they had committed abomination? nay, they were not at all ashamed..." Jeremiah 6:15.

"Woe unto them that call evil, good, and good evil..." Isaiah 5:20

Romans 3:18: "There is no fear of God before their eyes."

2 Thessalonians 2:11: "And for this cause God shall send them strong delusion, that they should believe a lie."

"They're dabbling in real, devilish, rotten-to-the-apple-core stuff and they don't even know it. Don't you just love it? We can take the reader deeper and deeper and they won't even know what hit them."

Another devil said, "And I know this was addressed earlier, but I love talking about it. Dabbling in any kind of evil is like playing Russian roulette with a person's very mind and soul. And I am happy to report that there are probably only a handful of parents who would say no to our garbage. And a preacher who would dare to teach about the hidden messages of my books to a captive congregation in a Sunday morning service is unheard of. If they talk about it all it's in a Bible study where the people that may need to learn about what it may do to their children just do not think it's important enough to show up. I love it.

"Think of the children that are reading these books. They look up to Harry. To some he is their idol. So, at some point in their lives, they will remember that it is okay to lie and cheat and swear and not respect authority and murder and even commit suicide. And it's okay to die, because, after all, you just live on and on in another life. They also get the idea that witchcraft is something that could get their curiosity up to try some of the things that Harry and the characters did in the Harry Potter books.

"Harry Potter has become an introduction to Wicca from the very young on up. And the movies will bring to life the story plot, with all the practices that the children have familiarized themselves with from the book.

"Make no mistake about it. Harry Potter books are about real, practicing witches and wizards, and their practices of divination, necromancy and sorcery. Harry's world is the world of witchcraft through and through!"

"I love it!!" exclaimed Satan. "Tell me more."

"I must say," the devil continued. "I have made this Scottish divorcee, Joanne Kathleen Rowling, a very wealthy woman. She almost fits the description by the prophet, Nahum: 'Because of the multitude of the whoredoms of the well favored harlot, the mistress of witchcrafts, that selleth nations through her whoredoms, and families through her witchcrafts.'—Nahum 3:4

"I am so glad that nobody pays any attention to that verse and also what the Bible says in Revelation 18:23: 'For thy merchants were the great men of the earth; for by thy sorceries were all nations deceived.' They probably haven't read in the dictionary that sorcery is witchcraft.

"And now I have Rowling create a brand new book called The Casual Vacancy for adult reading. Her comment in one news article was: 'Death obsesses me. I can't understand why it doesn't obsess everyone.' That should be a red flag right there that the author of the Harry Potter books is deep into dangerous, pagan, witchcraft beliefs.

"Of course death obsesses her because we've got her believing that it's okay to commit suicide, or murder someone, which evolves into the reincarnation cycle where you never die, you just live on and on in another life, as so well portrayed in the children's Harry Potter books."

With a big smile on his face Satan said, "Decent people sure are easy to manipulate. I love it!"

The devil assigned to the Harry Potter books said, "Funny you should say that, I inspired J.K. Rowling to put those very words, 'Decent people are easy to manipulate,' in Harry Potter and the Goblet of Fire somewhere; I think on page 676."

Satan said with zealous pride, "Now that we have let the cat out of the bag with Harry Potter and witchcraft 101, it gives me great pleasure to announce that there are real practicing witches that have real Wiccan churches that have tax exempt status by our government. It's classified as a real religion.

"I love that word, religion. Religion comes in all shapes and sizes and degrees and it has so many people all over the world deceived. But that's just the first step.

"My goal is to take them deeper and deeper and deeper to the next levels. We will never reveal where they will really end up. Little by little I want to harden their hearts so the real truth of God —the truth that will set them free— cannot get through. I want to keep them busy-busy-busy pleasing me day and night. Then it will be just a matter of time before many will self-destruct."

11

SATAN'S ULTIMATE EVIL

It wasn't long and I felt a strong desire not only to expose New Age and the Harry Potter books, and religion deceptions but I felt there was still more. I cried out to God, and God heard me. Just like it says in Psalm 18:6: "In my distress I called upon the LORD, and cried unto my God: he heard my voice out of his temple, and my cry came before him, *even* into his ears." The Lord knew that my cry was not for a new car or house. It was for a lost, religiously deceived soul. It was then that He took me on a journey I will not soon forget.

It all started one evening, at a Youth for Christ fundraiser, in a huge gymnasium packed to capacity. My husband and I "just happened" to sit across from an older gentlemen, by the name of Alfred Thompson. He told us about the deception of the NIV Bible. I couldn't believe what I was hearing. For a while I was almost angry at what he was saying. I thought: "He is talking about the NIV that I myself have used for years. He is talking about my NIV Women's Devotional Bible with the beautiful pink flowers on it." But the Lord didn't seem to care what the front of my Bible looked like. It was the contents He was concerned about.

After a while the feeling got so strong I didn't seem to have any peace, unless I was almost every day comparing the NIV verses with the King James. My husband bought me a parallel Bible for my birthday and that made it even easier. It didn't seem to matter how much I tried to forget what the gentlemen had said, I kept getting this feeling that I needed to research this even further. The Lord led me to 2 Timothy 2:15: "Study to shew thyself approved unto God, a workman that needeth not to be ashamed, *rightly dividing the word of truth." Rightly dividing* —comparing the two Bibles side by side. And sure enough Mr. Thompson was right.

Then I remembered Galatians 1:6-12, where the apostle Paul said that if anyone preach from what he referred to as the other, perverted gospel, let them be accursed. When the Lord showed me what that really meant, my heart went out to so many denominational pastors that I knew who were preaching from the perverted NIV. I didn't want them to be under a curse.

So I decided to just have a little, friendly talk with them about the things in their own NIV that was not right. Now, I thought they would be glad I was sharing this with them. But just the opposite happened. All of them first just gave me "the look" like, "Who do you think you are?" And then I would hear comments like, "I see nothing doctrinally wrong with the NIV." Another pastor said, "There are a few verses that kind of concerned me, but that's as far as I care to go." Another pastor said, "I don't really like the TNIV, but I do like the NIV." Another pastor said, "If I spend all my time worrying about which

Bible I preach from I will never get anything done." Another said, "I would never say anything contrary to the NIV."

Another made the excuse that, "The entire verse is in the footnotes." Another said, "You just don't know your Greek." I wanted to say, "You mean the ones from the ungodly Westcott and Hort?" But the icing on the cake was the day a young gentlemen approached me so excited because the youth group in his church had memorized the most NIV verses in the district. I wanted to ask him if they memorized the footnotes, too. But, of course, I didn't.

After all those negative comments, I felt like, "What's the use?" I just wanted to forget it all and not rock the boat, not make waves. But the Lord wouldn't let me think that for very long. I would be on my lunch break at work, and there would be a word or sentence in a newspaper that would jump out at me, and I would quickly write it down. I would be driving in the car listening to a Christian radio or CD, and I would scribble some words on a paper.

In my prayer time, there would be verses I was compelled to write down and save. I would wake up in the middle of the night and half asleep write down words and short sentences and more Bible verses. And then the rest of the night I slept like a baby. When I would wake up the next morning I couldn't believe all the things the Lord had me write down the night before.

The Lord led me to not only numerous Christian websites researching the deception in the NIV Bible, and many religions, and Harry Potter books, and New Age, but also homosexuality, and abortion.

My desires became stronger to expose these counterfeit

Bibles and religious deceptions. But how could I even begin to? I didn't have a theology degree. Abortion practices and homosexuality were just starting to come out of the closet. What did I know? When the thought would come to me I would pray about it. But I just didn't seem to be getting any answers. No big revelation. No big, ten-foot tall angel visited me. But for some reason I didn't give up. I felt like I couldn't give up. And then the familiar verse came to me in Proverbs 3:5-6: "Trust in the Lord with all thine heart; and lean not unto thine own understanding. In all thy ways acknowledge him, and he shall direct thy paths."

And then the Lord led me to Philippians, the 3rd chapter. When I got to verse 15, my eyes became glued on the words: "God shall reveal this even unto you." Tears welled up in my eyes. I felt so humble as I read the words "even unto me." And from that day on, "reveal" He did.

Through some Christian websites I learned some interesting but very disturbing things about Zondervan publishing company, licensed distributor of the NIV.

The following is from an article by Jay Klopfenstein in The Christian News, Dec. 20, 1993, p. 20.

Zondervan Corp., once a respected Christian publishing firm, Grand Rapids, Michigan, became a public company via a big initial public stock offering some 15 years ago. This was about the same time the NIV Bible was published by an outfit in New York called the International Bible Society, which financed the project. They then gave Zondervan Corp. the exclusive rights to the publication of the NIV version of the Bible.

After the initial offering, the stock's price rose

moderately but later the price fell sharply and many investors lost money. In 1985, a New Jersey investor filed a lawsuit which said he was induced to buy Zondervan stock because of false statements the company made to the Securities and Exchange Commission (SEC). In 1989 it was widely reported in the press: "Zondervan Corp. of Grand Rapids, Michigan, reached a $3.57 million out-of-court settlement with investors who contend they lost money when irregularities were found in the religious publisher's financial records."[3]

I didn't want to believe the very first sentence I read: "Zondervan, *once* a respected Christian publishing firm...." I always thought Zondervan promoted Christian values. At least that's the idea you get when you look on their own website under Zondervan Mission, Values and Publishing Philosophy:

OUR MISSION: To be the leader in Christian communications meeting the needs of people with resources that glorify Jesus Christ and promote biblical principles.

So why would someone call Zondervan a "once" respected Christian publishing firm?

For the next few weeks I prayed and prayed asking the Lord to help me understand why that was said. I thought maybe this was just some fly-by-night website. After all, you can't believe everything you read on the internet. And then one day the Lord led me to the following website,

http://truthinheart.com/Zondervan.htm

And this is what it said in big, bold letters:

"'Largest' Christian Publisher, Zondervan, is a Division of

---

3) A complete archive of this article can be found under the heading, "NIV Owner Big Pornography Publisher" at http://archive.today/3iIk9.

HarperCollins, which Publishes the Satanic Bible."

I thought, "The satanic Bible?" That just can't be! This is getting stranger all the time.

The Bible says in Luke 4:1, "Test the spirits." So I decided to check it out further. I went to Zondervan's own website: www.zondervan.com and clicked on, "About Us," and then, "History." And when I scrolled down to 1988 there were the words "Harper Collins." [4]

Zondervan History:

1931 – Zondervan is founded as a bookselling company in the Grand Rapids suburb of Grandville, Michigan by brothers Pat and Bernie Zondervan.

1933 – *Women of the Old Testament*, Zondervan's first book, is published.

1973 – Zondervan first publishes the New International Version (NIV) New Testament in partnership with the International Bible Society.

1978 – Zondervan publishes the complete NIV Bible.

1986 – The New International Version of the Bible, for the first time, **overtakes** the King James Version as the #1 Bible translation.

Notice the word, "overtakes" the King James Version.

And then I saw it with my own eyes:

In **1988** – Zondervan becomes a company of HarperCollinsPublishers, one of the world's largest publishing companies.

So then I went to Harper Collins Website and typed in the words satanic Bible in the search box thinking that no way is

4) http://archive.today/XLWfc

this true. But sure enough. With my own eyes, there, in plain sight, I saw Anton LaVey's Satanic Bible that Harper Collins has had for sale since 1976.

Also on their website was an NIV book called Harmony of the Gospels which was described as newly revised for students of the New International Version. They also had witchcraft and gay and lesbian books right along with Bibles and even children's books.

Someone once said, and this is so true: "Christianity began as a personal relationship with Jesus Christ. But then it moved to Athens, and became a philosophy. When it went to Rome, it became an organization. When it spread throughout Europe, it became a culture. When it came to America, it became a business!"

If you think this is bad, hold on to your hats. It gets worse.

2 Timothy 3:13: "But evil men and seducers shall wax worse and worse, deceiving, and being deceived."

Bear with me as I explain.

Then the Lord led me to the preface of my NIV Bible where there is a statement about stylistic consultants that states:

A sensitive feeling for the style does not always accompany scholarship. Accordingly, the Committee on Bible Translation submitted the developing version to a number of stylistic consultants. Two of them read every book of both Old and New Testaments twice —once before and once after the last major revision— and made invaluable suggestions. Samples of the translations were tested for clarity and ease of reading by various kinds of people —young and old, highly educated and less-well-educated, ministers and laymen.

So now, according to the NIV preface, think about it. You

are getting a mish mash of denominational, man-made ideas, of liberal religious traditions from various kinds of people making "invaluable suggestions" for the most important book in the world, The Holy Bible!

Now, allow me to tell you about these "various kinds of people," one in particular who was, believe it or not, asked to be an NIV "stylistic consultant."

Through these Christian websites[5], I learned that there was a practicing lesbian by the name of Virginia Mollenkott who was invited to be what they called a "stylistic consultant" on the NIV Bible translation committee.

One day I wrote to this lady, Virginia Mollenkott, and asked her some very direct questions. We wrote back and forth many times. The following are my questions to her, and next are her answers to me from many emails I received from her.

I sent my first email to her on February 10, 2008.
Dear Ms Mollenkott,

I have some questions that I would like to ask you. Some of which are a little personal, so if you don't want to answer them, I will respect your decision. I understand you were on the NIV Bible translation committee. Is that true? What exactly did you do on that committee?

Why is the word, "sodomite" completely removed from the NIV?

Why is the verse about Sodom and Gomorrah deleted from Mark 6:11 in the NIV?

What does the following verse mean to you in Leviticus 20:13: "If a man also lie with mankind, as he lieth with a woman, both of them have committed an abomination:

---

5) www.jesus-is-lord.com, www.purewords.org,
   www.lovethetruth.com, www.Biblebelievers.com

they shall surely be put to death: their blood shall be upon them."

Why is the precious Lord's Prayer in Luke 11 so chopped up?

Why are the words in Luke 4:8, "Get thee behind me, Satan," missing completely in the NIV Bible?

Why is angel changed to an eagle in Rev 8:13?

In John 14:2, why is our mansion in heaven changed to just rooms?

Why are the words, "take up your cross, through his blood, conviction, repentance, and the precious name, Lord Jesus Christ," removed completely in some verses or put in some footnote that no one bothers to read, anyway?

How can we "...hear the word of truth, the gospel of our salvation and be sealed with the Holy Spirit of promise," (Eph. 1:13), and, "receive instruction to hear the words of the Lord," (Jeremiah 35:13); and be, "doers and hearers of the word," (James 1:23); and, "meditate day and night on the word," (Psalm 1:2); and "...hear all the words that the Lord commands us," (Joshua 1:8); and in Deuteronomy 12:28: "Observe and hear all these words which I command thee, that it may go well with thee, and with thy children after thee forever?"

Speaking of children, my daughter has a Rainbow-colored Kids Devotional Bible NIrV (New International Revised Version). I noticed that there are even fewer footnotes than the NIV, so my child is getting very little of the true meaning and message of the Word of what God intended her to read and learn and meditate on and hide in her heart.

My concern is: what are my grandchildren and your grandchildren going to be hearing, or, worse yet, not hearing in the future NIV Bibles when the NIV is: "... perverting the words of the living God," (Jeremiah 23:36); and when, "Satan comes and taketh the words away," in Mark 4:15.

Every man, woman, and child on the face of this earth knows what Jesus said on the cross: "Then said Jesus, Father, forgive them; for they know not what they do. And they parted his raiment, and cast lots."

*Why would the NIV have a footnote for those words in Luke 23:34 that says: "Some early manuscripts **do not have** the sentence, casting doubt, did Jesus really say that? Like the Devil said to Eve in Genesis: Did God really say that? "Hath God said?"*

Why would a so-called Christian Bible publishing company, Zondervan, be connected in any way, shape, or form with the publishing company, Harper Collins, that sells the satanic Bible?

I don't think our human mind could ever grasp what eternity really means. I heard somewhere a definition of eternity. Picture a bird on a huge sandy beach. He picks up one grain of sand and flies it around the world a million times. Then he picks up another and another and flies each one a million times around the world. When he has cleaned the beach of all the sand, that's how long the first day in heaven or hell will be. Eternity is a long time to spend somewhere. In Hebrews 11 it says this world is not our home —we are just passing through.

We need to be about our Heavenly Father's business and be watchmen and expose the evil and warn the people that they need to repent and get right with God. Eternity is a long time to spend somewhere.

In Jesus service,
Judy

Now the following is her first email to me dated Wed., 13 Feb 2008 15:01:15 -0600 and also a combination of other emails she sent me.

Dear Judy,

I was a Stylistic Consultant on the New International Version during the entire time the translation was underway.

Dr. Edwin Palmer, the executive secretary of the International Bible Society Committee on Bible Translation, and coordinator of all translation work on the NIV Bible, heard me speak at William Patterson University.

Dr. Palmer respected my integrity and my knowledge and invited me to work on the NIV. Dr. Palmer always sent me the batches of manuscripts to review, and I always returned them (with my comments) to him.

My job was to read the manuscripts and make suggestions if there were places that contemporary readers might not understand —in other words, to be sure the English was clear and contemporary.

Being naive about the millions of dollars that these greedy publishers stand to make, I often worked for free, just out of my love for the Scriptures. It wasn't Zondervan's fault that I sometimes turned down my big $5.00 an hour stipend.

It never occurred to me at the time that Zondervan-IBS was going to get very, very rich on the NIV, etc. I guess it dawned on me when I had heard that the NIV is the pew Bible in the prestigious "chapel" at West Point Military Academy.

I have a letter thanking me for my work on the NIV when the project was completed. I also have the slip-case version sent out to the whole NIV team in 1978 by

Zondervan; and I have the tenth-anniversary edition sent out to the whole team in 1988 by the International Bible Society.

I myself have been lesbian all my life. I was told by the "still small voice" that God wants only happiness for me. I thank God for making me who I am and for loving me just as I am.

If you trust me enough to send me your street address, I will send you some informative information about the Bible, Science, and Homosexuality that will answer some many more of your questions.

I have a variety of Bibles which I check against one another, trying to come up with the clearest, most loving and balanced interpretation I can get. My Ph.D. is in English language and literature, so I am aware of style.

I feel as if everything I do and say is under God's direction, so that I am in constant contact with the Holy One.

Sodom was destroyed for its lack of hospitality to strangers (greed and cruelty to others).

But in recent centuries, people have used the word "Sodomite or perverts" as if it refers to homosexual men.

I presume that the NIV translators wanted to be accurate instead of pandering to recent inaccurate word usage.

Having known some of the NIV translators, I would say that the reason they put the footnote on Luke 23:34 is that the statement is true. Why should it matter to your faith if some versions included and some excluded Jesus or what he supposedly said, "Father forgive them, for they don't know what they are doing?"

My faith wouldn't really be destroyed if it turned out that the entire Jesus story was a beautiful myth: the point for me is that God has given us a picture of what

*Unconditional Love looks like, has told us that Jesus'
way is the way we children of God are supposed to live.
That's enough for me.*

*Translation is a difficult art: perhaps you should learn
a different language and then try to say EXACTLY what
you mean first in English and then in French or Arabic
or Chinese. You would discover that some nuance
always seems to get lost when you translate. The Old
Testament is written in Hebrew; Jesus spoke Aramaic;
most N.T. authors wrote in Greek.*

*Whenever you see differences in the NIV from other
translations, you can be sure the translators made the
changes because they felt they were getting closer to
what the original text probably said. No other reason.*

*Most translators are dedicated to being as truthful as
possible. The KJV was published in 1611, long before
copyrights were invented: the King's authorization was
the equivalent of a copyright. And anyway, it would be
in the public domain long since, which is why people
can reproduce it freely. It has nothing to do with "the
true Word of God."*

*The footnotes you see are attempts to be honest about
what is in the many early texts that often differ from
one another. I am confident that the NIV translators did
their best to be as accurate as is humanly possible.*

*Children cannot be expected to understand the difficul-
ties of translation; hence there are fewer footnotes in
the children's NIrV Bibles.*

*Whether God has rooms or mansions for us does not
bother me one bit: I'm quite sure heaven is beyond my
wildest imagination, better than anything I could ask or
think, and it is in the loving nature of God that I trust.*

*The Satanic Bible is not a book for worshippers of Satan;
it was given that unpleasant title by feminist Elizabeth
Cady Stanton, who was angry that the Bible was being
used to keep women secondary to men. So she put
together all the Bible verses that honor women, left out the
ones used to put women down, and angrily called it what
she knew male supremacists would think of it: "Satanic."*

*My advice to you would be to learn Hebrew or else
Greek and Aramaic, or all three, and study some of the
earliest biblical documents on your own.*

*I feel sure that Zondervan and the NIV Bible transla-
tion committee produced the most honest, scholarly
translation they were capable of producing. What would
help you most would be to read several scholarly books
about how the biblical canon was brought together over
a period of centuries.*

*Right now, my partner Suzanne and I face having to
leave our lovely home and pare down our possessions
and move into an assisted living facility; but every day
I pray that I am satisfied to be anywhere because now
God goes there with me. So I am not upset, just looking
forward to the next part of life's adventure.*

*The Bible tells us that we live in God and God lives in us
(see Acts 17, for instance); and if we believe that, as I do,
then everything that lives is holy. Including you. Including
your husband. Including me. God loves you and everyone
else equally much; you are safe. When you get to your
REAL home, heaven, there will be only Love to greet you.*

*Your sister in Christ,
Virginia*

"Your sister in Christ?" I don't think so! And her advice telling me to learn Hebrew and Greek and Aramaic, or all three

—I would have loved to have written back to her and asked her which Hebrew and Greek she is referring to that I should read. Is it the counterfeit manuscripts of the sly foxes, Westcott and Hort, that, by the way, believed in the theory of Darwin more than the inspired Word of the living God? Check it out yourself. Google Westcott and Hort versus Christianity.

Lesbian Mollenkott was a stylistic consultant on the NIV Bible Translation Committee. Could that be why there were verses changed to make the NIV homosexual friendly?

There is a website still available where you can see Ms. Mollenkott in a video at Harvard Divinity School at Harvard University.[6] As if what she says all the way through her lecture is not sickening enough, towards the end she said Jesus was genetically female all His life. She implied Jesus was a cross dresser. It made me sick to watch it and how she was mocking and making fun of the only One that could save her from an eternity in hell. God loves everyone as John 3:16 so states.

God doesn't send anyone to hell. They send themselves by the ungodly choices they themselves make. I am still praying for her. I care about her and all homosexuals and how deceived they really are.

The Bible warns that there would be those who would corrupt the Word of God (2 Corinthians 2:17), and handle it deceitfully (2 Corinthians 4:2).

From just a very small sampling of words and all the verses that were really changed, it's very evident that the NIV Bible has a long history of corrupt Bible translators. Now let me add

---

6) See the "Religion and the Feminist Movement Conference - Panel III: Virginia Mollenkott," found at https://www.youtube.com/watch?v=WjdD5-GGSEc.

that I don't believe that all the Bible translators of today deliberately set out to make a counterfeit Bible. But without the discernment of the Holy Spirit, these liberal, religious Bible translators were just copying what they sincerely thought were best manuscript sources.

I imagine their argument will be that no doctrine has been removed entirely. That is, there is still another verse in the Bible *somewhere* that teaches the doctrine. Oh really? So then you believe it is perfectly OK to remove a doctrine in one place as long as you do not obliterate it entirely? By this same logic, would it be OK with God if we removed the entire Gospel of Mark? After all, most of the doctrines taught in Mark are also taught in Matthew or Luke. No. This is faulty reasoning, and there is no excuse to remove even one word from God's words.

According to Galatians 1:11, in the King James, the Apostle Paul said, "But I certify you, brethren, that the gospel which was preached of me is not after man." That word, "certify," is only in that verse in the King James Bible. Certify, in the dictionary, means to confirm truth or accuracy of something. Wow! I would say that says it all.

Now today, we have these liberal, undiscerning, *religious* scholars playing with these counterfeit, corrupt manuscripts, adding their own brand of *un-certified* thoughts and words according to their religious, man-made traditions and beliefs.

When the Lord clearly said in Deuteronomy 4:2: "YE SHALL NOT ADD unto the word which I command you, NEITHER SHALL YE DIMINISH ought from it…"

Proverbs 30:6 reads, "ADD THOU NOT unto his words…"

And GOD'S LAST WARNING is Revelation 22:18,19, "…If any man SHALL ADD unto these things… And if any man shall TAKE AWAY FROM THE WORDS of the book of this prophecy, God shall take away his part out of the book of life." It was never about making the Bible easier to understand, or about the thee's and thou's and those so-called archaic words being removed to make it easier to understand. It was a clear and deliberate attack by the Devil to subtly, cleverly, change the Word of God and to do it in such a way that no one is the wiser. And besides, who would ever question a book with the words, "Holy Bible," on the front cover.

I find it interesting what is stated on the NIV Committee on Bible translation website http://www.niv-cbt.org:

"The Committee was established in 1965, and we continue to meet every year, under the terms of the NIV charter, to *monitor developments in biblical scholarship* and English usage and to reflect these developments in *periodic updates to the text.* The Committee is made up of leading evangelical Bible scholars *drawn from **various denominations*** and from some of the finest academic institutions in the world." (Italics mine.)

Various denominations is a red flag to me that these are from all walks of life undiscerning religious people (some from homosexual churches), changing and altering verses from the most important book in the world, The Holy Bible. Everyone has a right to love who they want but no one has the right to redefine marriage between one man and one woman.

The more that the Lord revealed to me, the more it became clear how and why a pastor I know can validate his daughter's lesbian marriage. With all the lesbian-friendly verses that are in the NIV, all anyone has to say is: "Well, it's in the Word of God; it's in the NIV Bible." This so-called man of God should be telling his congregation on a Sunday morning church service something like this: "You all have heard the horrible thing that has happened to my daughter. I love my daughter, but I do not accept what she is doing. Please pray that she will repent and turn from this sin. And please pray for me and our family. This has been hard on us."

But he doesn't say that. There is no conviction, no repentance. And the message of repentance and conviction is slowly being removed from the NIV.

Even though we don't know the day or the hour, God is winding things down in this world. He is giving people many subtle and not so subtle wake-up calls and opportunities to repent and be truly saved. The following true story is one of those wake up calls, that happened only a few hundred miles from where I live.

On August 19th 2009 at 2 pm in the afternoon there was a very interesting meeting that took place at the Minneapolis convention center in Minneapolis, Minnesota. The national ELCA (Evangelical Lutheran Church of America), was scheduled to consider a "Proposed Social Statement on Human Sexuality."

The issue was whether practicing homosexual behavior should disqualify a person from the pastoral ministry. Which then, very conveniently, opens up a Pandora's Box of validation for pastors to marry two ladies, or two men, or a lesbian, and a bisexual, and a straight person, or a gay, and a transgender or whatever suits their fancy.

God was not too happy with their meeting that afternoon and just a few minutes after two p.m., God sent a wake-up call to a very liberal ELCA meeting. On a day when no severe weather was predicted or expected, which baffled the weather experts, a tornado touched down just south of downtown Minneapolis, Minnesota and followed 35W straight towards the city center. It crossed I94 and hit the convention center where they were having this meeting, punching a hole in the Minneapolis, Convention Center roof.

Across the street from the Convention center was a very liberal Evangelical Lutheran Church that people were using for their worship services that week. The tornado split the church's steeple, causing the cross on top of the steeple to tip completely over, dangling in midair.

There were tents and tables set up outside the convention center to feed the people. The tornado stripped the tents, and turned the tables upside down. Kind of reminds me of the righteous anger Jesus had when He turned the tables upside down in the temple in Matthew 21.

I was sickened to say that the vote did pass 66.67 % (too close for comfort to the 666 mark of the beast) to allow what I would call the devilish spirit of homosexuality to be welcomed in every ELCA Church in America and opens the door to other churches and denominations to do the same.

The Christian Post commented:

Had Jesus Christ Himself come down from heaven and unfurled His white, heavenly robe before the entire assembly to reveal all the secrets of the universe, and had He lovingly addressed the ELCA assembly, telling the pro-gay lobby that they were mistaken in their interpretations of the scripture, that homosexuality should not be un-sinned, but that His death on the cross covers the sin of homosexuality, and to repent and be saved, some learned theologians from an esteemed ELCA seminary would have interpreted Christ's visit in a manner consistent with the outcome they desired. In fact, after the tornado hit, one GLBT (Gay, Lesbian, Bisexual, Transgender) advocate rose to proclaim that the upside down cross on the cathedral steeple was a sign that the Holy Spirit was blowing through the assembly in big ways as they embarked to do a "new thing.[7]

Bishop Michael Ingram is now confident that the Anglican Church of Canada will soon be blessing same-sex marriages and ordaining practicing homosexuals as ministers. He sees no problem in rewriting the Bible, the basis of the Anglican religion, so that its teachings will conform to the wishes of the activist homosexuals.[8]

The American Family Association had this to say:

"As confusing as homosexual advocates try to make this issue, Bible-believing Christians had better get used to such verbal sleight-of-hand. And they had better prepare themselves to it, because the arguments of "gay" advocates are creeping into virtually every denomination."[9]

Speaking of gay advocates, there was a man by the name of Bishop Spong, a gay bishop who has been on Oprah Winfrey's and other TV talk shows. This Bishop Spong was asked to be a speaker at a huge, prestigious, Gustavus Lutheran College on April 8, 2008.

I wrote to a spirit-filled, born-again, Christian pastor and asked him if he knew that this Bishop Spong was going to be speaking at this college. This was his email back to me:

---

7) http://www.christianpost.com/news/tornados-tempests-and-schism-in-the-elca-40530/ Aug. 27 2009 10:30 AM EDT

8) http://www.americantraditions.org/Articles/LIBERAL%20 REVISIONISTS%20PRESENT%20FALSE%20HISTORY%20 AND%20MORAL%20DECAY.htm

9) http://www.afajournal.org/2004/january/104warping.asp

The Bishop Spong stuff is not new to me. He has been an out-of-the-closet, wacko, left-wing, liberal for over 30 years. It's a travesty that he is welcomed on any Christian college campus, and to tell you the truth, if a college welcomes him to speak as if he is a legitimate Christian theologian, that college is simply not Christian anymore. I don't know how to tell most Lutherans about Bishop Spong. Most ELCA Lutherans are asleep in the pews, and wouldn't understand the concerns for him speaking at any Lutheran College.

This is posted on this Gustavus Lutheran College's own question and answer website:

"Q&A is a student-led campus group concerned with fostering a supportive environment for GLBTQ persons, as well as their allies. We seek to raise awareness regarding GLBTQ persons and their desire to simply be treated as equals, nothing more. We also strive to let those students on campus, who may be in the closet or struggling with these sorts of issues, know that they are not alone, and that we are one possible resource and/or outlet available."

The website is referring to the Gay, Lesbian, Bisexual, Transgender and I have no idea what the Q stands for. I wrote to this college and asked them what Bible translation they use at the college. This is the e-mail I received:

From: Rachel Larson <rlarson@gustavus.edu>
Subject: Bibles
Date: Tue, 18 Mar 2008 11:54:37 -0500

Hi Judy:

Thanks for contacting the college regarding Bible translations. We use the NASV in our worship service and our professors seem to like the NIV. For my own study, devotion, and sermon preparation I use the Harper Collins

Study Bible. The footnotes and cross references are very helpful. Hope this helps....

Chaplain Rachel

"Faith is... the confidence that it is okay to yearn and that when we yearn deeply there is a God shape to our hope and that God is real." —William Loader

Chaplain Rachel Larson
Gustavus Adolphus College
800 West College Avenue
Saint Peter, MN 56082
507-933-7450
rlarson@gustavus.edu

Notice that Chaplain Rachel Larson and the professors who like the NIV use the Harper Collins Study Bible. I am sure she hasn't got a clue what the NIV is, or the Harper Collins Study Bible that came from the same company that sells the satanic Bible as found on:

http://www.harpercollins.com/books/9780060786847/
HarperCollins_Study_Bible__Student_Edition/index.aspx

http://www.harpercollins.com/search-results/?search-term=satanic+bible

For the time will come when they will not endure sound doctrine; but after their own lusts shall they heap to themselves teachers, having itching ears; And they shall turn away their ears from the truth, and shall be turned unto fables, 2 Tim 4:3 4.

Please understand, I am not knocking any reputable Christian Bible publishing company that wants to make a companion study book to the King James Holy Bible. But when a Bible publishing company like Zondervan refers to their company as glorifying Jesus Christ and promoting biblical principles, I question how they can state that and then stamp the words Holy Bible on the cover of their perverted Bible. That's where my feathers get ruffled. That's where I get a holy, righteous, anger and want to do what Jesus did when He went into the temple courtyard and turned the tables of the money changers upside down. Jesus wasn't popular then, and He definitely wouldn't be now.

I know this book is going to ruffle the feathers of many. But to that I say: "Good!" Maybe that will make you mad enough to check things out for yourself and not take the word of anyone. I cannot be concerned about what man thinks, because God and His Word is my final authority.

I find it interesting to note that Zondervan calls its publishing company, not Zondervan Publishing Company but Zondervan Publishing House.

In Proverbs 3:33 KJV: "The curse of the LORD is in the house of the wicked: but he blesseth the habitation of the just."

Proverbs 14:11 KJV: "The house of the wicked shall be overthrown: but the tabernacle of the upright shall flourish."

Proverbs 15:6 KJV: "In the house of the righteous is much treasure: but in the revenues of the wicked is trouble.

Proverbs 21:12 KJV: "The righteous man wisely considereth the house of the wicked: but God overthroweth the wicked for their wickedness."

I decided to write to this deceived, religious, Bible publishing company, responsible for publishing and selling the NIV at their headquarters in Grand Rapids, Michigan. The following were my questions:

To whom it may concern,

I have some questions and concerns about the NIV Bible. If this is a Holy Bible, why were homosexuals

*permitted to be stylistic consultants on the NIV Bible
translation committee? Homosexuality is clearly an
abomination to the Lord as stated in the following verse:
LEVITICUS 20:13: "If a man also lie with mankind, as
he lieth with a woman, both of them have committed
an abomination: they shall surely be put to death: their
blood shall be upon them."*

*And why is the last part of Mark 6:11 about Sodom and
Gomorrah deleted in the NIV? King James Bible, Mark
6:11: "And whosoever shall not receive you, nor hear
you, when ye depart thence, shake off the dust under
your feet for a testimony against them. Verily I say unto
you, It shall be more tolerable for Sodom and Gomorrah
in the day of judgment, than for that city."*

*On the front cover of your NIV Bible are the words
NIV HOLY BIBLE. My question is: if this book is what
it says it is, a Holy Bible, why are the words "holy
men," (2 Peter 1:21), "holy angels," (Matt 25:31), "holy
brethren," (1 Thessalonians 5:27), "holy prophets,"
(Rev 22:6), "holy apostles and prophets," (Rev 18:20),
changed to just the words "men," "angels," "brethren,"
"prophets," "apostles and prophets" in the NIV?*

In Jesus service,
Judy

After sending my email three times I finally received a response:

*Date: Tue, 11 Mar 2008 13:35:36 -0400 (EDT) From:
Response (Carrie Colter) 03/11/2008 01:35 PM*

Thank you for contacting Zondervan.

*The International Bible Society will be better able to
answer your question due to that they own the translation rights to the NIV.*

You can contact them by calling 800-524-1588, or by going to www.ibs.org.

Thank you
Carrie

Okay, but what about Zondervan's part in all this? Something just didn't seem right. According to their website, "Zondervan's mission is to be the leader in Christian communications meeting the needs of people with resources that glorify Jesus Christ and promote biblical principles."

Biblical principles? Glorifying Jesus? When they remove the blood and cross and repentance and my precious Lord Jesus Christ not once, but over 25 times? I hardly think so!

So, one day I wrote to Zondervan again and fired off this question to them: To whom it may concern, Would you know why all the major key doctrinal changes in the NIV?

And this was Zondervan's email back to me:
From: "Zondervan Customer Care" <zondervan@ mailnj.custhelp.com>
Date: Tue, 14 Apr 2009 09:30:45 -0400 (EDT)

Subject: question

Thank you for contacting Zondervan,

Zondervan only has the publishing rights to the NIV translation. The International Bible Society/STL owns the translation rights.

These missing verses are part of what has become known as the "missing verses." These verses, however, are not really missing. They are included in the footnotes on the same page of your NIV Bible.

During the exacting translation process for the NIV Bible, some verses were found not to be included in the oldest or most reliable manuscripts that the NIV translators had available to use. Most of these manuscripts were not located until after the King James Version was first translated. When those verses could not be verified by the more reliable or older manuscripts, the NIV translators moved them to a footnote to reflect greater accuracy. People who grew up with the King James Version might feel that something has been taken out. The real question is not why these verses were left out, but more of who added them originally?

The reason some verses appear with a footnote while others are in a footnote is based on the level of certainty on the part of the translators on which the verse in question comes from the original text. If the scholars were more certain that the verse was not in the original text, the verse is placed in the footnote. If the scholars were less certain, the verse was placed within the text with an explanatory footnote added. It was all done to achieve maximum accuracy and readability.

Please be assured that your NIV Bible is accurate and reliable.

Additional information on the translation process and use of footnotes is located in the preface of your NIV Bible. For further information, you may also want to visit the International Bible Society's web site at www.ibsstl.org.

If you have further questions, please don't hesitate to write, or call one of our knowledgeable Customer Relations Representatives at 1-800-727-1309 on weekdays from 8:00 a.m. to 5:00 p.m. Eastern Standard Time.

Sincerely,
Carrie Colter

Zondervan Customer Care
www.zondervan.com

Then I fired off this letter to the IBS International Bible Society:

To whom it may concern,

Why all the major key doctrinal changes in the NIV (Holy Bible)? You were a very important part of history, making doubly sure there were only top prestigious scholars translating the very Word of God into modern day Bibles, checking and rechecking their credentials.

Making sure that these translators are not just any undiscerning, religious, fly-by-night, liberal, scholars but making doubly sure that these translators were born-again Christian translators, holy men of God filled with the Holy Spirit so they could discern the Holy Word of God from the perverted counterfeit manuscripts.

Jeremiah 23:36: "...ye have perverted the words of the living God..." Why?

In Jesus service,
Judy

I sent several emails and received no response from IBS, that I understand now, has merged with a company called Biblica in Colorado Springs, Colorado.

I never understood why the King James Bible was so popular for over 400 years; and why Satan tried so hard to destroy it and why he had so many people tortured and killed because they had it in their possession and preached from it. Now I am beginning to understand why.[10]

2 Timothy 3:16 tells us that, "All scripture is given by inspiration of God."

---

10) For more information, see "Another Bible, Another Gospel" by Robert M. Barker, online at http://www.jesus-is-lord.com/another.htm

2 Peter 1:19 tells us that the Word of God is authoritative and we, "…do well to take heed unto it."

2 Peter 1:20 indicates that the scripture has only one interpretation and it does not mean "whatever we want it to mean."

2 Peter 1:21 also tells us that the scripture came from God Himself as the Holy Spirit of God moved upon holy men and revealed to them God's Word.

Matthew 5:18-19 indicates that every letter in God's Word is perfect (the dots of the i's and the crosses of the t's). Compare Galatians 3:16.

Revelation 22:18,19 indicates that the curse of God will come on any person who adds to or takes away from the words of the Bible.

George Orwell's 1984 prediction may have been 30 years early but the world it envisions has arrived. Welcome to the new America. God has allowed a strong delusion to take over this nation (2 Thess. 2:11).

1 Corinthians 4:14: "I write not these things to shame you, but as my beloved sons I warn you."

Acts 20:31: "Therefore watch, and remember, that by the space of three years I ceased not to warn every one night and day with tears."

Galatians 1:6-7: "I marvel that ye are so soon removed from him that called you into the grace of Christ unto another gospel: Which is not another; but there be some that trouble you, and would pervert the gospel of Christ."

Satan did the same thing in the Garden of Eden to Adam and Eve. He perverted the Word of God. And he is still at it.

"Satan cometh immediately, and taketh away the word that was sown in their hearts," (Mark 4:15) (Luke 8:12). Satan, the father of lies, (John 8:44), "...the author of confusion," (1 Corinthians 14:33), is "...transformed into an angel of light," (2 Corinthians 11:14), and deceives the whole world," (Rev 12:9), corrupting the word of God," (2 Corinthians 2:17), handling the word of God deceitfully, (2 Corinthians. 4:2), "...perverting the words of the living God," (Jeremiah 23:36), "...making the word of God of none effect," (Mark 7:13).

Jesus Christ said, "...the words that I speak unto you, they are spirit and they are life." (John 6:63) Removing or adding to Jesus' words results in preaching "another gospel," which is not the gospel of Jesus Christ. Paul implies that preaching another gospel leads people to receive "another Jesus" and "another spirit." (2 Corinthians 11:4) 1 Peter 1:23-25 shows that there is a direct correlation between the preaching of the pure Word of God and spiritual regeneration: "Being born again, not of corruptible seed, but of incorruptible, by the word of God, which liveth and abideth for ever,...and this is the word which by the gospel is preached unto you."

The prophet Amos spoke of a day in which there would be a famine of hearing the words of the Lord (Amos 8:11). Today, man-centered messages and experiences have largely replaced the expository teaching of the Word of God. Often missing from the gospel presentation are vital doctrines of the Christian faith, such as the cross, the blood atonement, genuine faith, repentance, sanctification, and judgment.

Many in the church are busy serving, like Martha, but few are hearing Jesus' words, as Mary did (Luke 10:38-42). Deprived of the Bread of Life, many who profess to be Christians, have an outward form of godliness but, perhaps unknowingly, do not possess true spiritual life.

Throughout the Church Age, the Word of God has been preserved in the Textus Receptus, which is found today in the Authorized King James Version. The glory of our rich inheritance of truth in the Sacred Canon is slowly departing from the Church, and doctrinal confusion reigns. These things should not be so, "For God is not the author of confusion, but of peace, as in all churches of the saints" (1 Corinthians 14:33).

When the Jews at Berea were confronted with the gospel, "…they received the word with all readiness of mind, and searched the scriptures daily, whether those things were so." (Acts 17:11) They were commended by God for examining the Scriptures themselves in order to "Prove all things," (I Thessalonians 5:21). Like the noble Bereans, those who desire to know the truth today will study the Scriptures to determine which Bible faithfully preserves the doctrines of the Christian faith.

With all these devious, subtle, perversions going on now, I shudder to think what the Devil has planned for the next generation to memorize and meditate on and hide in their hearts. And not a moment too soon.

In 2005 Zondervan came out of the closet with another gender-friendly Bible, the TNIV, called Today's New International Version which cleverly, subtly, removed some masculine words, like men, man, his, him, and he.

For example, in King James, Matt 4:19: "And he saith unto them, Follow me, and I will make you fishers of men."

In Matthew 4:19 (TNIV): "Come, follow me," Jesus said, "and I will send you out to fish for people." Lesbians would rather read about "people" in their Bible. Never a masculine figure like the word "men."

And next is a real clever thing that the Bible translators did. This takes a little explaining. First, reading in the public-domain, no-copyright-needed, King James Bible in Hebrews 2:17: "Wherefore in all things it behoved him to be made like unto his brethren, that he might be a merciful and faithful high priest in things pertaining to God, to make reconciliation for the sins of the people."

So we see in the King James the words like unto his *brethren*. Now the NIV comes along in the late 60s early 70s and states, "For this reason he had to be made like his brothers in every way, in order that he might become a merciful and faithful high priest in service to God, and that he might make atonement for the sins of the people."

Notice the word brethren is subtly, cleverly, changed to "brothers" and also the words "in every way" are cleverly added, getting the reader used to reading and hearing the word, "brother," and the words, "in every way."

Now the TNIV shows up out of nowhere in 2005 making Jesus look like He could be a masculine or feminine figure:

Hebrews 2:17: "For this reason he had to be made like his *brothers and sisters in every way*, in order that he might become a merciful and faithful high priest in service to God, and that he might make atonement for the sins of the people."

Bingo! Now all that these deceived homosexuals have to do is go to the so-called Word of God with the words Holy Bible on the outside cover and with all assurance and certainty blurt out the words, "See, it's in the Holy Bible. "If Jesus can be a *man or woman*, I can too, so back off!"

You can't even find the words "*brothers and sisters*" once, in the King James.

The TNIV has the words, "brothers and sisters," plastered all over it 130 times.

There isn't any legitimate Greek manuscript in the universe to justify the addition of the word "sisters."

The TNIV removes 'he' over 1090 times.

The TNIV removes 'him' over 1600 times.

The TNIV removes 'his' over 290 times.

In January, 2005, Zondervan was once again in the news with its TNIV after initiating a $1 million advertising campaign and approaching *Rolling Stone* magazine with an ad for the "hip" Bible. *Rolling Stone*, long the bastion for free speech and often outrageous content, refused the ad, believing its audience would not appreciate a Bible advertisement. News of the refusal sent shockwaves throughout the magazine's readership and beyond. As *Rolling Stone* faced angry readers and advertisers, Zondervan benefited from numerous publications clamoring to show their political correctness and carry ads for the TNIV. In the end, *Rolling Stone* caved and Zondervan had a plethora of media outlets for the controversial TNIV.

We all remember the sex scandal back in 2006 with Ted Haggard. I am not angry at him or want to put him down. I am angry at a real, devilish power that convinced him to do this, even though it was his choice. And it sure didn't help any that the NIV and TNIV Bibles have so validated the homosexual lifestyle, with some key doctrinal words removed, like "sodomite," "conviction," "repentance," and "without natural affection," and many more.

There is a web page that I saved years ago from Zondervan Publishing Company website: Zondervan.com. It has since been removed. It is Ted Haggard endorsing the perverted

TNIV Bible complete with his picture. He states: "I have a passion for making sure today's generation hears God's Word in its most clear and accurate form. The TNIV assures that today's English reader will get the message, understand it, and be able to apply its transforming power to their lives." —Ted Haggard, President, National Association of Evangelicals; Senior Pastor, New Life Church.

I just don't understand how anyone could validate and endorse a lifestyle that God clearly calls an abomination. I always wondered how this Ted Haggard, President, National Association of Evangelicals; Senior Pastor, New Life Church or any so-called man of God, could compromise their convictions and ever make the conscious choice to cross over that line.

How can a pastor, behind closed doors, steal from the church nursery fund? How does it get to that point where a person submits to that "one little thought:" "Go ahead. No one will know." Could it be (and it grieves me to say this), that they are under a curse for validating and preaching from these perverted Bibles? They are not hearing from the living God anymore. And where do you hear from the living God? In His Word, and His Word only. Only God's Word has the certified seal of approval. Only from God's Word would the Christian Bereans allow the Apostle Paul to preach to them.

Acts 17:11: "These were more noble than those in Thessalonica, in that they received the word with all readiness of mind, and searched the scriptures daily, whether those things were so." The Christians in Berea searched the scriptures daily. That is how important it was to be in the living Word of God and not that other gospel.

And we make the excuse that: "Well, if I preach from this

Bible maybe it will make it a little easier for some to understand." And at some point I wondered about that myself. So
I asked the Lord what's up with that. And he took me to the
book of Jeremiah, chapter 36. God is giving the prophet, Jeremiah, revelation and inspiration to write a portion of the Word
of God, which is today the book of Jeremiah.

God tells Jeremiah to write on a scroll warning the people of
Judah if they didn't repent of their sinful ways they will be destroyed. King Jehoiakim hears only part of what Jeremiah wrote
and gets convicted of his own sinful ways and rejects it. The
king angrily takes a pen knife and cuts up, not just the part he
heard, but the entire scroll that God had told Jeremiah to write.

As hurtful as it is to talk about what happens in Jeremiah
36:23 with the king destroying God's Word, even more hurtful is what happens in v. 24: "Yet they were not afraid, nor rent
their garments, neither the king, nor any of his servants that
heard *all these words*."

It was no big deal to anyone. There was no remorse whatsoever. No one stood up and said, "This is so wrong. God loves
us so much that he is just trying to warn us before it's too late."

How sad! Rather than the king admitting he and his people were sinning, King Jehoiakim destroyed God's promises of
forgiveness and safety for himself and his people.

So when the king burned the precious Words of God in the
fire, he thought that was the end of that, they are gone forever.
He didn't know that no matter who destroyed God's Words
they would be preserved somehow, somewhere forever.

God had it all covered. He told Jeremiah to write the same
scroll all over again. Jeremiah was disappointed that the king
and his people had not truly repented. Now think about this.

Did Jeremiah tell God, "How about if I change what You want me to write? Let me remove the words 'conviction' and 'repentance,' or many other key, doctrinal words. Let me make it easier for him to understand. Maybe then the king and his people will repent if I change it the way I want to. Please, God, let me scratch what you said and put it into my own words. Maybe I could make my own way to get the King and his people saved." Did he do that? No! He wrote exactly to the letter what God said: If they didn't repent they had their warning and they were destroyed.

And in verse 28 the Lord tells Jeremiah, "Take thee again another roll, and write in it *all the former words that were in the first roll*, which Jehoiakim the king of Judah hath burned." Notice the Lord didn't say you can change a few words here and there. No, He said to write all the words that he was given before the king destroyed them. So, all the words are very important to God. That's why He said don't change them.

In Jeremiah 26:2, "Thus saith the Lord; Stand in the court of the Lord's house, and speak unto all the cities of Judah, which come to worship in the Lord's house, **ALL** *the words that I command thee to speak unto them;* ***diminish*** *not a word:*"

David meditated on ALL God's works (Psalms 143:5). Joshua 1:8: To "...meditate therein day and night, that thou mayest observe to do according to ALL *that is written* therein:" Deuteronomy 12:28: "Observe and hear ALL *these words* which I command thee, that it may go well with thee, and with thy children after thee *for ever*, when thou doest that which is good and right in the sight of the Lord thy God."

The Apostle Paul said, "ALL *scripture* is given by inspiration of God, and is profitable for doctrine, for reproof, for correction, for instruction in righteousness." (II Timothy. 3:16). "All scripture" does not mean a little here and a little there. It means "All scripture." Jeremiah said that the "The wise men... have rejected the word of the LORD; and what wisdom is in them?" (Jeremiah. 8:9)

But is it any different today? Like the king, people will read a little bit, and when it starts getting convicting and a little too close to home, they make the excuse it's just not for them. And they cut and paste and recreate a message that won't convict, that will validate any lifestyle and religion.

People today don't want to get their toes stepped on; they want to be entertained and pampered and pacified. They want to be treated like a king. And if they say a little sinner's prayer and swear or backslide a little, it's no big deal. Again the Lord says, where is the "trembling at my words?" (See Isaiah 66:2.)

That king and his people had been warned many times. This was not the first. God gives everyone the opportunity to get saved.

There are pastors I know that would never preach from the TNIV but they don't think twice about defending the NIV and preaching from it. Now, don't get me wrong. They may quote a Bible verse from the King James but then back to the NIV they would go —to the other gospel in the counterfeit manuscripts the Christians in Berea and the Apostle Paul would have nothing to do with.

And speaking of the TNIV, there were some discerning Christians like, for one, James Dobson from Focus on the Family, who said that the TNIV is wrong.

Dobson noted in a prepared statement to Baptist press, Feb. 6, 2002:

"I have now received sufficient feedback from a large number of evangelical scholars to convince me that this new work is a step backward in the field of biblical translation. Accordingly, I am now adding my name to the list of those who disagree with the liberties the International Bible Society has taken with God's Word in the new translation.

"I love the Scriptures and I know them to be the very words of God to His creation. Like most evangelical Christians, I want my Bible to contain an accurate translation of the canonical Hebrew and Greek texts. Accordingly, I will continue to speak out against any effort that alters God's Word or toys with translation methodology for the sake of 'political correctness.'

"It is particularly unfortunate that the IBS has now chosen to go its own way." Baptist Press clarified by saying IBS withdrew its endorsement of the 1997 Colorado Springs Guidelines for Translation of Gender-Related Language in Scripture, "developed in the wake of controversy over IBS plans, at the time, to introduce a gender-neutral Bible in the U.S. market by 2001."

According to Dobson, the IBS, "risks dividing the Christian community again, as well as damaging its own reputation and undermining the wonderful work in which it has been engaged for more than 150 years."

I would like to write to Mr. Dobson and say that's all fine and dandy that you are exposing the TNIV, but I have a news flash for you: the NIV and 2011 NIV are just as perverted and corrupt.

I wrote to Zondervan and asked them if they were going to

be selling the TNIV Bible. And this was their email back to me:
  "Thank you for contacting Zondervan.

  I am sorry, but the TNIV Bible will be going out of print. Zondervan will not be reprinting."

  Thank you
  Zondervan Customer Care

Now because James Dobson and others gave the TNIV Bible translators so much grief, this perverted book is going by the wayside.

But did that stop Zondervan? No way! They just convinced some undiscerning, liberal, religious, Bible translators to tweak the TNIV a bit and make a brand-new, hot-off-the-press 2011 NIV. In it we have Jesus, not like his brothers and sisters in every way, but now he is "fully human." In Hebrews 2:17 (NIV 2011) it reads: "For this reason he had to be made like them, *fully human in every way*, in order that he might become a merciful and faithful high priest in service to God, and that he might make atonement for the sins of the people."

By saying "fully human," that verse can mean whatever a liberal, religious, pastor wants to make it mean. The sky's the limit.

So the TNIV is no longer being printed. But did the Devil raise the white flag and surrender? No way. He made sure there was a backup. What the Lord showed me is that in the same year, 2005, that the TNIV came out of the closet, another Bible also came out of the closet. It's called the "New Century Version" by Thomas Nelson, Inc. This Bible again implies that Jesus can be a man or woman.

Hebrews 2:17 (New Century Version) "For this reason Jesus had to be *made like his brothers and sisters in every way* so he could be their merciful and faithful high priest in service to God. Then Jesus could die in their place to take away their sins." All this, even though Jesus was born a baby boy. Does the Bible say: "For God so loved the world that he gave his only begotten (sister or brother or son or daughter or fully human being," or does it say, "His Son?" The changes play right into the Devil's hand in his desire to make a homosexual-friendly Bible.

And now let's look in the King James in 1 Timothy 3:16: "And without controversy great is the mystery of godliness: God was manifest in the flesh, justified in the Spirit, seen of angels, preached unto the Gentiles, believed on in the world, received up into glory." Just look what the undiscerning, religious, NIV Bible translators really did to that same verse in the NIV, TNIV, 2011 NIV. They have the undiscerning nerve to change "God" to just "he." 1 Timothy 3:16: "Beyond all question, the mystery of godliness is great: He appeared in a body, was vindicated by the Spirit, was seen by angels, was preached among the nations, was believed on in the world, was taken up in glory."

And also the New Century Version: "Without doubt, the secret of our life of worship is great: He[a] was shown to us in a human body, proved right in spirit, and seen by angels. He was proclaimed to the nations, believed in by the world, and taken up in glory."

Of course we have a footnote that everyone refers to: (Ha Ha!)

Footnotes: 1 Timothy 3:16 **He,** Some Greek copies read "God."

The Devil is also laughing at: "He appeared in a body…," So what? Everyone has "appeared in a body." The statement does NOT even make sense. The NIV, TNIV, and now 2011

NIV and the New Century Version distort I Timothy 3:16 into grammatical nonsense. They take the deity away from God and put just the word "He" in that particular verse.

I find it ironic, and very disturbing, that these new, easier-to-read Bibles invent ways and mis-translations to quickly remove the "masculine word 'he'" in hundreds of places to appease the feminist and yet, they insert the "masculine word He" in 1 Timothy 3:16 when the reference is the clearest reference to the deity of the Lord Jesus Christ in all the Bible! If there's one doctrine that Christians should guard and protect it surely is the deity of our Lord Jesus Christ. Satan hates the fact that Jesus Christ was God manifest in the flesh.

And then there is one little change that happens right under our noses in the NIV-TNIV -2011 NIV treatment of John 14:2 —something very odd.

First, in John 14:2 in the King James: "In my Father's house are many mansions: if it were not so, I would have told you. I go to prepare a place for you."

Then in John 14:2 in the NIV, "mansions" are changed to many "rooms:" "My Father's house has many rooms; if that were not so, would I have told you that I am going there to prepare a place for you?" Notice that *question mark* at the end. The 2011 NIV Bible translators knowingly, deliberately, change the sentence from declarative to interrogative. The Lord Jesus Christ is no longer issuing a statement of "fact" and "truth," —now it's a question!

Does that remind you of any other verse in the Bible? How about Genesis 3:1? "Now the serpent was more subtil than any beast of the field which the LORD God had made. And he said unto the woman, Yea, hath God said…?" Ah, so, the master of the question mark —Satan, "Yea, hath God said?"

The serpent's little, subtle, question mark in Genesis 3:1 triggered the fall of mankind. Just that little element of doubt.

The first "question mark" in the Bible is from the mouth of Satan [serpent]. And it "questioned" the Word of God. Hmmm.

If you go on Bible gateway.com (which by the way is promoted by Zondervan), and click on NIV, which is now the 2011 NIV, you will see the question mark plain as day in John 14:2: "My Father's house has many rooms; if that were not so, would I have told you that I am going there to prepare a place for you?" The NIV 1984 is the original NIV which doesn't have the question mark.

So with all the discerning, born-again Christians that, bless their hearts, stood up and spoke up and said, "This is not right," Zondervan had no choice but to stop the presses on the TNIV. But it was not soon enough, the damage has been done.

So, as you can see, the Devil doesn't put his hands up and say, "Well, I'm done! They got me." No, he convinced these religious Bible translators to make a new Bible that they call, what else, but the 2011 NIV, and just on the anniversary of the 400-year-old King James Bible. How quaint! But it's almost a carbon copy of the NIV-TNIV.

With every updated, new and improved NIV they removed a few more key doctrinal words and just a few more masculine words like man, men, his, him. Out of the NIV came the TNIV which removed even more masculine words.

Now the 2011 NIV removed even more. Like the words "man" 1334 times, "men" 544 times, "his" 1311 times, and "him" 1286 times.

Luke 8:12, "...then cometh the devil, and TAKETH

AWAY the word..." And now we have our modern-day, un-discerning, religious, liberal, evangelical, Bible-translating scribes. The Lord warned us in His word, in many times over, about these religious, perverted, century-old, and modern-day scribes.

Matthew 22:29: "Jesus answered and said unto them, Ye do err, not knowing the scriptures, nor the power of God."

Jeremiah 23:36: "...for ye have perverted the words of the living God."

Jeremiah 8:8: "How do ye say, We are wise, and the law of the LORD is with us? Lo, certainly in vain made he it; the pen of the scribes is in vain."

Mark 12:38: "And he said unto them in his doctrine, Beware of the scribes, which love to go in long clothing, and love salutations in the marketplaces."

Mark 1:22: "And they were astonished at his doctrine: for he taught them as one that had authority, and not as the scribes."

Mark 11:18: "And the scribes and chief priests heard it, and sought how they might destroy him: for they feared him, because all the people was astonished at his doctrine."

Luke 19:47: "And he taught daily in the temple. But the chief priests and the scribes and the chief of the people sought to destroy him."

Luke 20:46: "Beware of the scribes, which desire to walk in long robes, and love greetings in the markets, and the highest seats in the synagogues, and the chief rooms at feasts;"

Matthew 23:13: "But woe unto you, scribes and Pharisees, hypocrites! for ye shut up the kingdom of heaven against men: for ye neither go in yourselves, neither suffer ye them that are entering to go in."

Matthew 23:27: "Woe unto you, scribes and Pharisees, hypocrites! for ye are like unto whited sepulchres, which indeed appear beautiful outward, but are within full of dead men's bones, and of all uncleanness."

These modern religious scribes seem to hate Jesus. The truth is offensive to them. So, they found a way to either delete the name of Jesus, or Lord Jesus Christ, or they would cleverly hide them away in some confusing footnotes that no one bothers to read to this day.

There is one thing I am noticing more and more: the King James Bible exalts the Lord Jesus Christ. There is no book on this earth which exalts Christ higher than the King James Bible.

Jeremiah 6:16: "Thus saith the LORD, Stand ye in the ways, and see, and ask for the old paths, where is the good way, and walk therein, and ye shall find rest for your souls. But they said, We will not walk therein."

I wrote this email to Zondervan in 2012:
From: pauljudy777@bevcomm.net
Subject: NIV Bible

I am confused. Some Christian book stores say that you have the 2011 NIV Bible and others have never heard of it. Can you explain.

This was Zondervan's reply back to me received: 6/15/2012 9:08 AM:
RE NIV Bible CRM00096374

Thank you for contacting Zondervan.

The 1984 edition of the NIV is now out of print, and almost all the NIV's that are in the stores now is the 2011 edition. There are exceptions like the NIV

Archaeological Study Bible, and the Large Print NIV
Life Application Study Bible.

Thank you, Zondervan Customer Care

So, now this 2011 NIV is being sold in Christian book stores all over the world. It's the master of deception. And speaking of the master of deception, it reminds me of a true story that happened to me.

When I was a little girl my father was an alcoholic. I can remember my Dad would think it was cute to play tricks on me. My dad would hide store brand bread in the brightly-colored, red-, yellow-, and blue-ballooned Wonder Bread wrapper. I would be eating my supper and Dad would take a piece of the store brand bread out of the Wonder Bread wrapper, and butter it for me, knowing full well it was not Wonder Bread. I would say "this bread tastes funny." But Dad would always lie, and tell me, "It's the Wonder Bread you like."

As not to make any trouble, I said nothing. But for some reason, it just didn't taste like the good, fresh bread that I had remembered having before. But then, who was I to question it? Dad kept feeding me this holey, burnt, bread. If that wasn't bad enough, one day my father came to the supper table with a toy for me. It was a gray, rubber knife that he had gotten at the dime store when he went up town to get his cases of beer. Mom let me play with it at the supper table to take my mind off how awful Dad was acting. With my little toy knife I tried to cut the burnt crust off my holey bread but it just kept bending and the more it bent, the more my drunken Dad would laugh, not with me, but at me.

And then one day I came in from playing outside and I caught my Dad putting the store brand bread in my Wonder

Bread wrapper. I shouted, "Dad what are you doing?" I can remember as if it was yesterday.

The smell of liquor was on my Dad's breath as he was weaving back and forth and slurred out the words, "I wanted to see how long it would take before you realized what I had done." Like the fox said to Little Red Riding Hood, "The better to deceive you my child."

And then it dawned on me, that's exactly what the father of lies, old Satan himself, is doing and has done. He is just dulling the powerful sword of the Spirit to a child's gray rubber knife, biding his time to see how long he can deceive people, before they wake up in their sleeping churches. For centuries the Devil has used unholy scribes and then modern day liberal, religious, Bible translators to secretly poke holes in the good, sweet-tasting bread of life, burning it just a little here and there.

Everyone has been sold a bill of goods that the NIV Bible is the real bread of life because it is put in a NIV wrapper with the words "Holy Bible" somewhere on the cover.

And speaking of attractive covers, you should see some of the new, 2011 NIV Bibles. They have very inviting, attractive-colored covers, with colored flowers. These are referred to as the bloom collection Bible. The words NIV and of course the words Holy Bible are etched in the sides of the NIV Bible.

I asked the lady that worked in a Christian book store if she knew of any changes in the new NIV Bibles and she took me to Psalms 1 and read: "Blessed is the one who does not walk in step with the wicked or stand in the way that sinners take or sit in the company of mockers."

She said that "blessed is the man," has been changed to

"blessed is the one…." And then she said with a big smile on her face, "This is more gender friendly." I could feel my blood start to boil as I felt like saying something almost mean to her. Then I thought, "I can't do that. It would not be right."

The word "men" appears 3,222 times in the King James Bible. But in the gender-friendly, feminist, perversion of the NIV 2011, you'll only find the word "men" 1027 times in their entire Bible. Pretty sad, huh?

The word "man" appears 4,538 times in the King James Bible. But in the gender-friendly, feminist perversion of the NIV 2011, you'll only find the word "man" 1,989 times.

I noticed something else in the NIV 2011. There is nothing about a stylistic consultant in the preface, namely Virginia Mollenkott. And why not? Because they are done with her. They got just what they wanted from her. The damage is done.

In the King James Bible in Titus 1:2 it says, "God cannot lie." In the NIV, TNIV, and now the NIV 2011 it is changed to: "God does not lie." There's a big difference between "does not lie" and "cannot lie." It is certainly true that God does not lie; but Titus 1:2 goes even farther by assuring us that GOD CANNOT LIE, who has PROMISED eternal life before the world began.

Ezekiel 22:30: "And I sought for a man among them, that should make up the hedge, and stand in the gap before me for the land, that I should not destroy it: but I found none."

Now, like the TNIV got stopped in its tracks, how many discerning Christians are going to stand in the gap and send letters to the offices of the Committee of Bible Translation and Zondervan and get this perverted, counterfeit Bible 2011 NIV off Christian's book shelves?

One would have to have their heads buried in the sand to miss the sheer existence of demonic spirits. They have fueled wars, and attacked the home, the family, education, governments, churches; murdered millions of unborn babies in the mother's womb, interfered with human sexuality and the marriage relationship. Every good gift of God has been attacked by the Devil. Is it not strange then, to think that Satan would leave the Word of God alone?

From the centuries-old Dark Ages to the New Age, from Genesis to Revelation, the Devil and his disciples have attacked the precious Holy Word of God like no other book that has ever been written in the history of the world.

Proverbs 30:6: "Add thou not unto his words, lest he reprove thee, and thou be found a liar."

Even the press knows not to mess with the Bible. The following was reported by Bible Believer's Bulletin: The Wall Street Journal and Newsweek both came down defending the King James Bible. They mocked at the marketing gimmicks used to try to push aside the KJV, and they called for the KJV to be restored as the world standard for Biblical authority...."

Here is a very useful quote from the Wall Street Journal: "To tamper with the King James Bible, based on some imagined manuscript evidence, is like adjusting Big Ben to somebody's private wrist watch."

Psalm 11:3: "If the foundations be destroyed, what can the righteous do?"

The line must be drawn where we say, "If the King James Bible was good enough for 400 years, then it is still good enough for me."

The King James Bible to me now is like a treasure chest of

precious nuggets that God reveals to me one nugget at a time. The Devil has people believing that it is so hard to read. "It's not hard at all if you really get to know the author. But there are also companion study books to the King James Bible available that *do not* deliberately remove or alter key doctrinal words of God.

The old archaic King James Bible has the 7-letter word "Saviour" with the letter U (you) in mind. The NIV has switched the seven letter word "Saviour" to the six-letter-word "Savior," reminiscent of the 666 anti-Christ who wants to be like the most High (Isaiah 14:14).

Revelation 13:18: "Here is wisdom. Let him that hath understanding count the number of the beast: for it is the number of a man; and his number is Six hundred threescore and six." This number of a man, 666, will have his fingerprints all over his Bible.

For example, the six-letter-Savior NIV Bible will state in Isaiah 63:8: He said, "Surely they are my people, *children who will be true to me*"; and so he became their **Savior**.

Now the King James in Isaiah 63:8: "For he said, Surely they are my people, *children that will not lie*: so he was their Saviour.

Notice how the message is cleverly twisted to children needing to be true to a six letter savior, the number of a man 666, the anti-Christ who wants to be like the most High (Isaiah 14:14).

Leave it to God to put His stamp of approval on the King James like we see in Galatians 1:11 where the Apostle Paul states very clearly: "But I *certify* you, brethren, that the gospel which was preached of me is not after man."

No way would the Apostle Paul ever preach from what he

called the other perverted gospel in Galatians 1:6-12.

The only Bible that people wanted to destroy and burn was the King James Bible. But as you have learned, God always found a way to preserve it forever: "The words of the Lord are pure words: as silver tried in a furnace of earth, purified seven times. Thou shalt keep them, O Lord, thou shalt preserve them from this generation forever." Psalm 12:6-7

The only Bible that has stood the test of time for over 400 years and has earned the right to have the words, "Holy Bible" stamped on the cover, is the King James Version.

There is so much at stake now —the authority, the accuracy, the inerrancy of the Holy Word of a Holy God. And if ever the Lord needed his people to take a stand for His Word and refuse to budge, it is now.

So with all this information that I have just shared with you and the many notebooks full of scribbled notes, and years of research I had transferred to the hard drive of my computer, I felt like I needed to do something with them. As the days and weeks and months went on, things seem to be falling into place. When I say fall, I mean literally. In December of 2011 I fell and dislocated my elbow. In July of 2012, I fell again and had to have ankle surgery complete with plates and screws.

There were people that told me horror stories of the pain that I would be in with the compound fracture I had in my ankle, but to God be the Glory, I had very little pain at all. With each accident I was out of work for several months.

I could do nothing but rest and recover and yes, you guessed it — write. With my Bible by my side and my laptop on my bed, my years and years of notes and Bible verses and numerous research I had saved on the computer, it started to become a

paragraph and then another and another until it became, sometimes, humorous and sometimes I could see it was a very serious
story.

Since I have been working on this story, I have developed a
film over not just one, but both my eyes. There are times that
I have to use a magnifying glass. And my husband had to increase the little cursor on the computer screen and even then I
had to magnify it more and strain and blink to see the words
on the screen at 200%. I have never had anything like this in
my life. The ophthalmologist told me I have a disease called
cornea dystrophy. And it will only get worse.

But I don't believe the report of that doctor. I believe the
report of the Lord and I let the Lord decide how much I will
be able to see. There are times when I just start to cry, I feel
so humble, knowing that the Lord has chosen me to write
this book. At times I would have so many tears in my eyes I
couldn't see what I was writing.

The older gentlemen that I told you about earlier, that told
me about the NIV, has a brother who goes to a church whose
pastor had a very negative encounter with the NIV. It was the
pastor's birthday and some of the people in his church gave him
this beautiful, leather-bound, NIV Bible. Most of the people
in his church already had the NIV so they wanted him to have
one, too. He said he put away his King James Bible and started
preaching from the NIV. He preached from it for over a year.
And every Sunday when he preached from it, he noticed less
and less salvations. He said the anointing was slowly leaving.

One day, he was doing a baptismal service preaching from
the NIV. His wife had her King James and tried following
along in the service. It was then she noticed that, when the

pastor was reading verses from the NIV, words were missing. He said that his wife told him: "It changed the whole story, the NIV changed the whole thing."

It was at that point that he put the NIV away and started preaching from his King James Bible again, and the anointing came back and good things started happening in his church again. And his last words were: "I will preach nothing but the old King James."

3 John 1:4: "I have no greater joy than to hear that my children walk in truth."

It's interesting what the great, old-time-revival, King James preacher, Charles Spurgeon said, "We must sharply grapple the *false doctrine*, driving the sharp hook of truth between its joints; we must clearly understand the error, and study the Word of God, so as to be able to controvert (dispute) it. The Devil and his allies will try to trick you into carrying their wares, but be warned in time, and reject their *vile devices*."— C. H. Spurgeon

Jeremiah 6:16 (King James Bible), "Thus saith the LORD, Stand ye in the ways, and see, and ask for *the old paths*, where is the good way, and walk therein, and ye shall find rest for your souls. But they said, We will not walk therein."

Do you think that Charles Spurgeon today would preach one word from a false-doctrine, a perverted gospel, that does not glorify the Lord Jesus Christ 100%, has not been certified, preserved by God Himself? Do you think he would preach from just any uncertified, fly-by-night, Bible version that has the six letter word Savior that liberal Greek scholars, and undiscerning, liberal, religious, Bible translators have cleverly, deceptively made it easier to understand?

Well, my husband has said in several different ways, "This is probably enough for people to digest right now."

And I came back with, "But there is so much more that the Lord has put on my heart. There is so much more I need to tell them." And he didn't say any more, he just gave me "the look" that made me finally say, "Okay, hon, I hear ya!"

Throughout this book I know I have stepped on toes and even gone where not many care to go.

"Am I therefore become your enemy, because I tell you the truth?" (Galatians 4:16) "I write not these things to shame you, but as my beloved sons I warn you." (1 Corinthians 4:14)

I know I am going to get people that will just not understand and will mock me. Some may be bitter and angry and even hate me. But if this book moves someone to prayerfully check out the information for themselves, and moves them to have a little talk with Jesus, and exposes just one more demonic spirit, that's all I ask, just one more soul, it's so worth it to me. Until I take my last breath here on this earth, until that day I go to be with Jesus, I will continue to do what the Lord has called me to do, to be His fruit inspector exposing that forbidden fruit, those...

Good-Ole Rotten Apples